T0089006

DICTIONARY
OF TORTURE

Nigette M. Spikes

abbott press

Abbott Press books may be ordered through booksellers or by contacting:

Abbott Press
1663 Liberty Drive
Bloomington, IN 47403
www.abbottpress.com
Phone: 1-866-697-5310

ISBN: 978-1-4582-1791-2 (sc)
ISBN: 978-1-4582-1792-9 (e)

Library of Congress Control Number: 2014916613

Printed in the United States of America.

Abbott Press rev. date: 12/19/2014

To Cody, Sara, and Sam, for whom I would
die a death beyond a thousand cuts

PREFACE

I'm not sure when it all actually started, but for as long as I can remember, I've always had a fixation on punishment. When I was about three, I would dream of skeletons acting like they were still alive, and when they weren't dancing, they were shut up in iron maidens and stretched on torture racks or torturing naked, living humans. Of course, I had no idea what the iron maiden or the rack was at that time. I believe those dreams were precognitive to what I would see and learn one day. When I was eleven, I visited my first torture museum, and waiting outside was the very first torture device I ever met—a chair of nails. It was big and rusty, and there was a dainty little sign resting on the arm restraints that read "Please do not touch the chair." I gleefully went in, and I memorized everything I could. Some of those things have made their way to the *Dictionary of Torture*, such as the fearsome breast ripper, the terrifying spiked collar, the pear of anguish, and the Judas cradle. Since then I have visited a few other torture museums around the country, but sometimes I would see a torture reenacted in a film and feel compelled to look it up online to learn more. Or I would read about torture in books, usually nonfiction, and learn from them, but often I scour the Internet and take notes. When I was fifteen, I came up with the idea of compiling all the information I'd been collecting and calling it the *Dictionary of Torture*. I have spent many more years learning and adding to the dictionary. Even though it is now finally here, I feel like I will never stop learning, and if I learn about a torture not included in this edition, I will want to put it in the next one. I want to teach everything I know about the subject because

I find it fascinating. Torture is an integral part of human history and reveals human nature for what it is underneath the social conventions that require us to act like normal human beings and not bloodthirsty, sadistic savages. Torture is universal, and even though it is frowned upon in modern times, it is still relevant. The human race will evolve and will probably invent new methods of torture in the future.

ACKNOWLEDGMENTS

I would like to thank my parents for their unconditional support and understanding.

INTRODUCTION

From the world's first documented society several millennia ago to every modern nation today, torture has been a part of human history and continues to remain present. Even in countries and cultures where it is illegal, it remains something to be practiced underground, albeit unsanctioned and often unwarranted. Torture is nonconsensual and is always against the victim's will. A person who consents to torture is *not* being tortured. That is not torture. It is like rape. In fact, rape is a form of torture and is a valid entry in this dictionary. But generally, no matter where or when, there were always two types of people who were torture victims—criminals and "criminals." Torture was originally intended to be used on criminals who deserved it, such as the thief who would get his hand amputated. Someone who had committed adultery would either be castrated or shunned. A murderer would be executed the same way he killed someone else who was innocent and didn't deserve to die. However, throughout history, especially in ancient Rome and medieval Europe, people in authority had a tendency to abuse their power to discriminate against people they didn't like or people who didn't fit into their mold as to who the ideal person was. During times when people were superstitious and paranoid and were not allowed to read the Bible for themselves, common people would accuse others of crimes they didn't commit simply because they didn't get along with them, and usually the accusers were believed. Even when there was no evidence, the people blamed would be publicly punished and executed. During the Spanish Inquisition, the priests and cardinals who enforced the Inquisition had license to burn anyone who was a heretic, meaning not Catholic, at the stake, but then the definition of the word *heretic* became so broad that even good Catholics were publicly destroyed by fire. Even women were considered heretics just for existing, but it seems as though no matter what region or era I study, there are certain people who tended to get hurt more than others. The top five most commonly tortured groups of people of all time include

1. women;
2. homosexual men;
3. non-Christians (pagans, savages, etc.);
4. those who were labeled witches; and
5. actual criminals and prisoners of war.

Many ancient societies considered women equal to or greater than men, but others, such as ancient Greece, Rome, and the Mongolian Empire were very patriarchal. When they conquered other nations, they spread their influences to them, and most of Europe and Asia became highly antifeminist until the last century. With the rest of the world (Africa, the Americas, Australia, and the Pacific Islands), women's places in society varied by tribe or group, or it depended on their status or who they were married to. In some places women had rights, but in others they were only considered property. In places where women were generally oppressed, they were more likely to become torture victims for things that were perfectly natural, like having a libido. Everyone had arranged marriages that didn't consider either the boys' or the girls' personalities or compatibility. In medieval Germany, there were certain tortures that were usually used exclusively on women, such as the breast ripper for adultery or promiscuity. The branks were used on women caught scolding their husbands in public. Muslim countries preferred to nip any and all sexual behaviors in the bud by inducing female circumcision in girls' early childhoods so they would not be tempted to commit adultery when they were married later in life. During the Spanish Inquisition, it was believed that women lost their souls when they had their menstrual cycles. Therefore, women were inherently heretics. A woman could've been burned at the stake just for having a menstrual cycle. Around the same time in Florence, Italy, there was an insane but widely influential monk named Girolamo Savonarola who condemned women just for being beautiful or for wearing cosmetics.

Coincidentally, societies that oppressed women enacted antisodomy laws, whereas societies that respected women tended to be tolerant of people with an inclination for sodomy, particularly modern societies but also some ancient Native American tribes, some ancient African tribes, and the ancient Celts. Although just about anyone can practice sodomy, some people are more famous for it than others, namely homosexual men. In the ancient and Middle Ages for the Mongolian Empire and Ancient Greece, sodomy with any kind of an implement was a prescribed punishment for generally heterosexual men for the act of adultery or incest. In Aztecan Mexico, homosexual men were executed by being burned internally as they were sodomized with ashes. In ancient Rome, a man could penetrate another man of a lower status than he was, such as a military man penetrating a common citizen or a general penetrating a lieutenant, and the emperor could have sex with anyone he wanted; however, if a man of a low status penetrated someone who was higher than he was, he would be publicly castrated, and the man allowing himself to be penetrated would commonly be disemboweled. During the Spanish Inquisition, homosexuality was considered a sign of sorcery, and men were punished as witches for it, usually with sodomy with an anal pear of anguish, disembowelment, castration, or burning. Isabella, a former queen of England, sentenced her homosexual husband, Edward II, to be burned internally to death by having his executioner put a red-hot spit inside his rectum. Under the reign of Henry VIII, sodomy was a capital offense, and those who were caught practicing it were beheaded or hanged. Sodomy and homosexuality remained illegal in Europe until the last century, although it wasn't usually a capital offense. In the Middle Ages throughout Europe, women were thought to not have libidos; however, in actuality they were not supposed to, and if they were found to have libidos in any way, they were tortured and burned, beheaded, hanged, or drowned. Because of this, lesbianism wasn't considered or commonly thought about until Victorian England and modern times. Like homosexuality or bisexuality in men, the same things found in women could be punished by imprisonment, or if they were of royal or noble blood, they were instead deemed insane and forbidden from being seen publicly.

Peoples of many ancient nations in which women were respected and homosexuality and bisexuality were tolerated, such as the ancient Celts, the Native Americans, and most Africans south of the Sahara, were persecuted in their own homelands by foreigners, driven away, and nearly destroyed. An example would be when ancient Rome conquered Britain and desecrated temples and religious artifacts and pillaged the people for gold and raped them. They did these things because they were greedy for power, land, and money. Many Celts and Anglo-Saxons, some of which included Queen Boudicca and her family, were captured and brought to Rome to die in the arena and were shown as laughing stocks. Later Romanized Anglo-Saxons made several wars with the Irish because of religion. At first they clashed because the Irish wouldn't practice the Roman religion and Romanize. Then there was conflict because they wanted to convert them to Catholicism, both of which were won by the English eventually. The ancient Romans persecuted all people who would not practice the Roman religion. Most people know that Christians were severely persecuted under the rule of several emperors, such as Caligula, Nero, and Diocletian, but Jews, Muslims, atheists, Gnostics, and anyone worshipping any deity other than any of the ones from the Roman pantheon were condemned, tortured in the arena, and martyred. In early Christian times, there was a group of Christians called the Gnostics, and after the Roman empire converted to Christianity under Emperor Constantine, the early Catholics felt that the Gnostics were a threat to them and their beliefs, although the reasons for their feelings are lost to us today. After Emperor Constantine converted to Catholicism, he was persuaded to persecute the Gnostics until there weren't any left of them. After all the Gnostic Christians were extinct, the Roman arena eventually fell out of practice. Centuries later there was a revival of Gnosticism throughout all of Europe. Those who practiced it in Western Europe were called Cathars; those who practiced it in Eastern Europe were called Bogomils after a prophet by the same name who brought about this revival. The medieval Gnostics themselves were peace-loving and against violence except to protect oneself, family, or property in self-defense. They never caused problems for anyone, and neither did the Jewish or Muslim communities they coexisted with; however, the Catholics, for reasons we don't know today, began persecuting people who weren't Catholic. This was the Spanish Inquisition, but despite its name, it spread throughout all of Europe. Although anyone who was Muslim or Jewish or who was thought to be a witch was persecuted, the real targets were the Gnostics, and they were persecuted to the point of extinction yet again. Also the Knights Templar, a secret society within the Catholic church, was suddenly and inexplicably persecuted, and many of them were rounded up, tortured, and burned on Friday, October 13, 1312. This was the birth of the superstition surrounding that date Friday the thirteenth. Some people believe it is when the devil himself walks the earth, not necessarily knowing the origin of this belief.

Before Christopher Columbus sailed to North America, other people had been there, such as the Vikings, and some scholars believe that the Celts, ancient Egyptians, and ancient Hebrews might have been there and established their own tribes or interbred with the natives who were there. If those things are true, they most likely did not chase the natives away from their homes and mistreat them. Most likely they would've tried to make friends with them and live off the land like they did. They would've been respectful and tolerant of the differences in religious beliefs and culture and would've avoided making war with them if possible. However, the medieval Europeans who came to North America felt differently. They dogmatically believed that their beliefs were correct and that their culture civilized. They persecuted Native Americans for their religious and cultural beliefs and also because of their skin tone and unique features that made them stand out from other races. Medieval Europeans believed that the Caucasian race was the superior race and that God made them more accurately in his image than anyone else. This was also reflected in religious artwork in which all Bible people were painted as being light-skinned with brown or blond hair and brown or blue eyes, even though they merely assumed that they looked like them and wouldn't have actually known. Similarly the ancient Greeks considered all those who were not native Greek speakers barbarians and inferior to them, and the ancient Romans considered all those who were not of Roman birth inferior to them. Ancient and feudal Japan considered themselves the most superior country and most superior, race and because of this, they shunned all other countries. Foreigners who went to Japan were either shunned or executed. The Japanese thought they were superior in all things until the eighteenth century when American and English businessmen convinced them to trade by showing them inventions like the telescope. Up until that point they thought they were most superior in all inventions, literature, customs, culture, and religion.

All the European settlers, whether English, French, Dutch, German, Spanish, or Italian, took away all the Native Americans' land. They fought and killed many of them, so countless tribes were destroyed, and they locked them up in reservations all because they felt justified in doing so. Because settlers believed that they were superior to all other races, they considered Africans animals, and they brought them over as slaves against their will. Nobles from Victorian England and mainland Europe at this time also owned African slaves and their descendants. The Victorian English also conquered India. Instead of trading them for goods such as tea and spices, they wanted to own them, and they felt it was right. When the Victorian English conquered Australia and New Zealand, they also persecuted the native Aborigines and Maoris the same way they persecuted the Native Americans. Dutch, French, and British settlers persecuted South Africans and took away their home similarly when they settled there. It seems that the right to discriminate against other people just for being different from them in both outward physical appearance and inward religious belief has always been a European characteristic.

Also a European characteristic that stems from ancient times but died out in the last century was the paranoia of people who practiced witchcraft. This started two millennia ago when ancient Romans tried to conquer Celtic Britain and Ireland and learned about their spiritual beliefs and rituals the Druids did concerning prophecy or spell casting to ensure things such as the protection of a person or object or the undoing thereof. The ancient Romans and Greeks considered them evil, barbarous, and crude, and the Celts worshipped a stag-headed god who later influenced what people thought Satan looked like. However, it was during the Spanish Inquisition when people first started to become paranoid of people practicing witchcraft to the point of obsession. Both men and women were accused of witchcraft or sorcery for anything and everything from having better crops or a better financial situation than a neighbor to homosexuality to a poor woman knowing how to read and write to a family member or neighbor dying under bizarre circumstances ... or what would've been seen as bizarre at that time. The medieval definition of a witch was a person who either practiced paganism or was believed to have worshipped Satan. A sorcerer or sorceress was someone who took it a step further and had sexual intercourse with him. It was thought that an unmarried woman who was pregnant was carrying his child, and she would be burned, hanged, or stoned for it. People who were accused of witchcraft were given a trial by ducking stool to see if they would drown. If they did, they were considered innocent. If not, they were tortured by things such as the chair of nails, which was at the time called the witch's chair, or the pear of anguish was put inside the vagina or anus and expanded so as to stretch out the orifice until pulverized. Also used was the witch catcher to keep a person at an arm's length but to lead him or her to and from a trial or site of execution. It was believed that if a witch touched a person, he or she would be under the witch's control. Any person showing any outward signs of insanity, such as hallucinations, grandiose delusions, bipolarity, or extreme melancholy, were thought to be possessed by a demon or under the spell of a witch, and they were either publicly shunned, banished, or locked away in their own houses or in prisons. The rest of Western Europe also suffered from extreme paranoia of witches. Hundreds of men were burned as witches in England under Queen Mary, who was a devout Catholic, but most of the men she sentenced to burning were Protestant and unwilling to convert to Catholicism. Colonial America was also fearful of witches, and many innocent men and women were drowned, hanged, and burned for it in New England. They were accused of witchcraft by people who would be considered insane by today's standards because they suffered from hallucinations and other signs of insanity.

Last but not least, a lot of people who were tortured and executed were actual criminals. Universally there are some people who are simply unwanted by society, such as murderers, rapists, thieves, and adulterers. In the most ancient times anywhere in the world, justice was very swift, and criminals were usually punished or executed on the spot. Beatings as either corporal or capital punishment were the most common, but there was also amputation and beheading. There are some punishments such as these that seemed to have been universally employed by all societies across time and space, and these were some of the first tortures; however, ancient Greece and Rome experienced a huge wave of new tortures previously not seen, such as the rack, the iron maiden, the first human press, the wheel, and several methods of burning someone slowly and sadistically. The Spanish Inquisition also saw a wave of new tortures, many of which were enthusiastically pioneered by Dominican monk Tomas de Torquemada and endorsed by Pope Innocent III, including the chair and bed of nails, the pear of anguish, the Spanish donkey, as well as new and improved versions of ancient Roman standards like the torture rack and the wheel. Generally each country in the Middle Ages had a particular favorite method of torture or execution that they were known for. The Spanish were all about burning people at the stake, while the English had been enthusiastic about flagellation since Celtic times (and it remained with them regardless). Ninety percent of all different types of whips were invented in medieval England. Because some ancient Celtic tribes settled in parts of France, they spread their love of flagellation to the ancient Gauls, and like England, medieval France practiced flagellation just as zealously. Many types of humiliation devices were invented in Germany. Turkey was known for impaling people, and most Muslim nations were also known for flogging; however, unlike Western Europe, they were particularly known for using canes on the soles of the feet as opposed to the back or buttock areas. China and Japan were known for using bamboo in their tortures, but the Japanese were famous for hanging victims upside down and burying them. The Chinese were also known for their water tortures, the thousand cuts, and similar punishments. India and Southeast Asia were most known for deaths by elephant. Most Native Americans would've preferred shunning or banishment above all else, although they were also famous for scalping and eyelid removal. The Aztecs and Mayans zealously preferred bloody human sacrifices by violently removing the heart with a hooked implement. Many African and South Pacific tribes preferred cannibalism. Most Native American tribes did not practice cannibalism. Only a couple of tribes did eat the corpses of the enemies they killed in battle as part of a religious ritual, but this did not happen frequently.

People who were prisoners of war were often tortured, and if a citizen of one country ventured into another with whom the first country had bad relations with, that person was at risk of being imprisoned and tortured just because other people were paranoid even if there was absolutely no evidence that the person was a spy or had any malicious intent. Three millennia ago the ancient Mayans and Aztecs would make war with other tribes for the sole purpose of capturing prisoners of war to use as human sacrifices if there weren't enough criminals of their own to execute in this manner. If an ancient Iroquoian lost a family member or spouse, the entire tribe went out on mourning wars in which they would make war with other neighboring tribes. They would bring back scalps to the mourning people as a way of cheering them up, but usually this didn't work. Then they would go battle again, but this time they would capture as many prisoners of war as possible. They would remove their fingernails and beat them, and they would take them to a gauntlet where they would be forced to sing and dance; however, they would be required to sing in Iroquoian, and it would be a very specific song and dance they did not know. The prisoners of war would be laughed at and humiliated. After this, they were forced to fight one another in a gauntlet as a way for the tribe to determine strength and stamina. Any man who fell and could not get up or could no longer fight would have his body burned and then have bucketfuls of water poured on him so his flesh fell off. The losers' intestines would be thrown into the river, and the ones still fighting were forced to eat the hearts. The grieving Iroquoian decided the winner's fate as to whether he should die a slow death by fire and be scalped or be adopted into the tribe to replace the missing relative or spouse. Other tribes such as the Comanche, Apache, Sioux, Arapahoe, Cheyenne, Blackfoot, Lakota, Shoshone, Bannock, Mojave, Yavapai, Crow, Kiowa, Kickapoo, Ute, and Chiricahua also put prisoners of war in gauntlets. They only put male prisoners in the gauntlet. In the plains tribes' version of the gauntlet, each man in the tribe formed two parallel lines only seven feet across from one another and were armed with clubs. Each prisoner of war was to run between the lines while avoiding getting hit. Very few prisoners escaped, and those who did were tracked down and brought back. These tribes tortured all prisoners all alike—man, woman, child, white, Hispanic, black, and Native. Whenever there was a torture session, it was usually led by a woman since a lot of these tribes were matriarchal. Every tribe member was required to participate in some way, even the children, or else they would be tortured as well.

In America during the 1950s after the bombing of Pearl Harbor, Caucasian Americans became highly suspicious of Japanese people, so much so that they became paranoid about all Asians, even if they were born an American or didn't even have Japanese blood. Asians living in America were rounded up and put into concentration camps, but unless there was any evidence of being involved in the Japanese-American war, they were not interrogated or tortured. Unlike the concentration camps of Hitler's Germany or the gulags of Stalin's Communist Russia, where anyone who was imprisoned was tortured and guaranteed to die a horrible death, people who were put in American concentration camps were simply locked away, and most of them were released five or ten years later. A lot of them were actually put there to protect them from other people who would hurt them because of misconceptions and paranoia at the time.

Hitler and Stalin's bloodthirstiness and high body count could only be rivaled by Vlad the Impaler, on whom the title character of *Dracula* was based. He was born Prince Vlad Dracule III of Wallachia, an ancient Eastern European country that is now modern-day Romania, Bulgaria, and some of south Poland. Wallachia always had uneasy relations with Turkey, and when Vlad was about eleven, a Turkish army invaded his father's castle and kidnapped him and several other members of the household. They were kept as prisoners of war in Turkey for about three years, and most of them died horribly during that time. As a prisoner of war, Vlad was routinely beaten, sexually assaulted, and humiliated. He saw the same treatments administered to his siblings and servants who were all captured with him. He saw many of them die by impalement. Turkey had been using impalement as a capital punishment for centuries; however, this method of punishment became forever fixated in Vlad's mind as his signature. As soon as he could go back to Wallachia, he became king. He immediately began punishing all criminals with impalement, although he was also known for sentencing people to burning and flaying. He did not discriminate against men, women, or children. He made war with neighboring countries frequently, but he especially targeted Turkey. He would either make prisoners of war into slaves or impale them. At one point when a Turkish army was heading to a battlefield to meet his army, Vlad had prepared approximately twenty thousand impaling stakes, and all of them had condemned criminals as victims. The Turkish army immediately fled the scene and surrendered, allegedly while Vlad was eating a meal and drinking either wine or blood. This incident became known as the "forest of the impaled." People began referring to Vlad as *Tepes*, which meant *Impaler* in Wallachian. Not surprisingly, a lot of people wanted Vlad dead, and he was imprisoned in Hungary, another country he made war with several times. Sometime during his last stay he died. There are no records as to how he died or when. Some people believe he was assassinated by beheading, but this is not certain. Most people generally believe he was about forty-five.

Even though in modern times the Western hemisphere has banned torture and execution is illegal in many places, torture is and always has been around and will continue to be. Someday when space travel becomes commonplace, we may execute people by throwing them into outer space naked or forcing them to go without oxygen. We may someday experience a new wave of torture in which new implements are invented unlike anything ever seen since ancient Rome, the Spanish Inquisition, or medieval England. Stamping out torture and execution completely will most likely never happen.

A

Abacination: The act of permanently blinding a person by removal, slitting, causing extreme damage to, or putting out of the eyeballs, damaging the optic nerve, or destroying the part of the brain that processes sight. Abacination most frequently occurred in history by putting a red-hot poker in the eyes. Sometimes red-hot coals are put in place of the eyeballs and the person burns to death. Abacination can also occur by **eyelid removal** and then burying people up to their heads or tying them to the ground face up so as to face the sun. Abacination can also occur by putting a knotted rope over one or both eyes and pulling it tight around the head sometimes with a cudgel acting as a crank until the eye(s) goes blind because of too much pressure. See **knotted rope**. *Samson was punished by abacination.* Origin: ancient Philistine.

Abdomen Strikes: To punch or slap a person in the stomach. *The boxer gave his opponent ten abdomen strikes.* Origin: ancient Mesopotamian.

Acid: A chemical that burns or dissolves skin on contact. Acid may be used on one particular body part, may be dumped on a person as an execution, or may be used to dissolve the entire body after death. *She was forced to lay there, unable to move while acid dropped on her forehead rhythmically every other second.* Origin: ancient Egyptian.

Ackerman's Hotel: Nickname for any kind of prison, originated with Newgate Prison in medieval London, England, but now is a general term referring to any prison anywhere. *A man named Ackerman was in charge of Newgate Prison once, and it became Ackerman's hotel. The clients couldn't ever check out except by death.* Origin: medieval England.

Admiral of the Red: Nickname for an executioner. *The admiral of the red executed many people.* Origin: French Revolution.

Affectionate Snake: A snake used for the purpose of sodomizing, a person so it disembowels the person inside by eating them, trying to escape. This is a variant of **rhaphanidosis.** *The homosexual died from having the affectionate snake make love to him.* Origin: ancient Chinese.

Agony Boots: Another word for **iron boots.**

Alfet: A cauldron in which to heat weapons and tools or to burn a victim. *The alfet heated the tongs.* Origin: ancient Anglo-Saxon.

Amputation: The act of cutting off a body part such as a hand, foot, nose, breast, ear, or other as a way of punishing and marking them as criminals for life. *The thief had his hands amputated.* Origin: ancient Hebrew.

Anal Pear: See **pear of anguish.**

Ankle Cuffs: See **shackles**.

Ankle Stocks: A form of stocks or pillory, a wooden board with two holes in it that ankles are locked into. The ankle stocks, just like any other form of stocks or pillory, opens from a lock to the side, and the top of it is lifted like a box. The circles for the limbs are then only half circles. *Ankle stocks are usually paired with foot whippings, canings, bastinado, and foot roasting.* Origin: ancient Hebrew.

Anna Grin: See **Glasgow smile**.

Anna Smile: See **Glasgow smile**.

Anodyne Necklace: Another name for a **noose**.

Apega of Nabis: Name of the first **iron maiden**.

Arena: A large scaffold where thousands of audience members plus the king or emperor watches victims, sometimes called gladiators, fight to the death, get eaten by lions or other animals, get tortured, and or get executed. Compare to **gauntlet**. *Emperor Diocletian put to death many Christian martyrs in the arena.* Origin: ancient Roman.

Asphyxiation: The scientific word for **strangulation**.

Australian Stock Whip: See **stock whip**.

Ax: A blunt, double-bladed, two-handed weapon used not only in combat but also to decapitate victim with their necks stretched out over chopping blocks. *Mary, queen of the Scots, was a famous victim of decapitation by ax.* Origin: ancient Roman.

B

Babe in the Wood: A nickname for a miscreant in a **pillory**. *The babe in the wood was put there for public intoxication.* Origin: medieval England.

Bamboo Torture: Putting a person where a bamboo seed is planted and restraining the person there. As the plant grows up after a number of days, it slowly impales the person. *The gardener killed the butler with the bamboo torture and then piled dirt around the sprouted bamboo tree to cover his crime.* Origin: ancient Chinese.

Banc de Torture: French for "frame of torture," this is their name for the **rack**.

Banishment: See **exile**.

Barrel of Shame: See **barrel pillory**.

Barrel Pillory: A barrel with a hole cut out on top so the victim can have their head sticking out. Some versions also had holes for the people's legs so they can walk in a parade of shame. Some had holes for the people's hands so they may be handcuffed in front of them for others to see. As an execution, the person was completely concealed inside with nails lining the inside of the barrel and then thrown off a cliff or rolled down a hill or the street. Furthermore, the ancient Romans would put a person in two barrel pillories stacked on top of each other, and the person would live the rest of his or her life, usually a fortnight, which was also an early form of **scaphismus**. *The barrel pillory was used to humiliate petty criminals who committed petty crimes such as stealing.* Origin: Spanish Inquisition.

Bascule: The pivoting plank of the guillotine or similar beheading device. *Marie Antoinette laid on the bascule and waited for death.* See **guillotine**. Origin: French Revolution.

Bastinado: The act of caning the soles or a person's feet as either a torture or an execution. As an execution, the person endures being canned for hours, but without the skin breaking, until the victim dies. *The vandal was bastinadoed since he could not pay the fine.* The word *bastinado* is Spanish in origin. The ancient Chinese were the first to take up this practice.

Bat: Another word for **riding crop**.

Batog: The act of two people straddling one person facing each other on either side of the victim's body while they are laying naked facedown on the ground. They use two sticks, rods, or batons to **flog** the person until a supervising referee tells them to stop. *Mistress Pain and Mistress Misery batogged Misty on her buttocks with dowels until Mistress Death decreed for them to stop.* Origin: medieval Russia.

Beating: To strike a person repeatedly and violently so as to hurt or injure the individual. *The men beat the woman to death with rods for adultery.* Origin: ancient Mesopotamian.

Becane: French nickname for the guillotine, called so because the word also applies to shunting engines that slid down rails like a guillotine blade.

Bed of Nails: An iron **rack** with nails people were made to lie down on. Other tortures could be added, such as stretching them or burning them with hot iron pans on their feet or other various places, putting a lighted candle to their sides, heating the nails, or other things. *Some cultures do not use the bed of nails for punishment, but rather they use this device to test individuals for divinity by seeing if they don't bleed.* Origin: ancient Roman.

Bee Basket: A large basket in which a person is put and is then lifted by a pulley system to the top of a tree branch where there is a beehive. The person is then stung to death. *Gregorius was allergic to bee stings so his death from the bee basket was relatively fast.* Origin: ancient Roman.

Beheading: The act of cutting off a person's head. *Mary, queen of the Scots, was a famous beheading victim.* Origin: ancient Hebrew.

Bell Collar: A collar with a bell either hanging over the victim's head or in front of the individual's neck. The person would be made to walk through the streets with the bell ringing at every move so everyone would know where they were. *The catty scold paraded through town, wearing a bell collar in a parade of shame so she never scolded again.* Origin: Spanish Inquisition.

Belting: The act of flogging or whipping a person with a belt. Compare to **tawse**. *The belt is not only an item of fashion. It is also a weapon, and that's the reason why criminals are forced to surrender them when incarcerated.* Origin: medieval Scotland, originated with the tawse.

Beyond a Thousand Cuts: The act of randomly selecting a body part out of a thousand or so possibilities and mutilating that body part and then repeating the process with different body parts until death, but if something gets cut off, that person is forced to eat it for nourishment by the executioner for the purpose of keeping the person alive to endure more punishment. Compare to **thousand cuts**. *Mar-Janah died by receiving death beyond a thousand cuts and she ended up eating and defecating one third of her own body.* Origin: ancient Mongolian.

Biblical Discipline: See **corporal punishment**.

Bicycle Pump: This modern invention can be used to pump air into the rectum with the intention of causing intestinal cramps. *The bicycle pump torture works best if the victim's anus is plugged afterward so they cannot fart out the injected gas.* Origin: The use of a bicycle pump as a torture device has been documented in modern China.

Bin: Chinese for "feet and kneecaps removed."

Birch: A bundle of leafless twigs from a birch tree, willow, other trees, or shrubs. *The birch is used for birching and comes from the birch wood tree.* Origin is Celtic England and Scotland, but the birch was used wherever the birch tree grew.

Birching: To flog or whip a person with a rod made of birch wood. *The vaudeville comedians birched each other for laughs.* Origin is Celtic England and Scotland, but birching was common wherever the birch wood tree grew.

Birching Donkey: See **riding the rail**.

Birching Pony: See **riding the rail**.

Birching Table: A type of **stockade** or **pillory** that is a board with two holes, one for each hand. *The birching table looks like a stockade with no hole for the head.* Origin: Celtic Scotland.

Birch rod: See **birch**.

Blackjack: A **blacksnake** with the load concentrated in the handle, it is usually a lead ball or steel ball bearing. *The disgruntled gambler whipped the blackjack dealer with his own blackjack whip.* Origin: modern United States.

Blackmailing: A psychological torture in which the torturer threatens victims with something against them in order to get a favor out of them, such as keeping a secret. *Trevor blackmailed Eric with a degrading photograph so he could help him bury his murder victim.* Origin: ancient Mesopotamian.

Blacksnake: A type of **whip** related to the **snake whip**. It is flexible and has a heavy shot load extending from handle to lash. *The blacksnake whip looks like a blacksnake when curled up.* Origin: modern United States.

Blade: A flat cutting edge on weapons or torture devices/instruments. *Many people think of a multi-bladed instrument such as a chair of nails when they hear the term torture device.* Origin: ancient Mesopotamian.

Blinding: See **abacination**.

Blood Eagle: The act of slitting a person's back on either side of the spine, pushing the individual's rib cage forward until it broke, pulling out the liver, and then leaving the person to die. It is called blood eagle because the liver throbs can look like an eagle's wings flapping as it soars in the sky. *Erik punished his enemies with the blood eagle.* Origin: ancient Norwegian.

Blood Letter: Original name for the **flying guillotine**.

Boats: See **scaphismus**.

Boat Sandwich: See **scaphismus**.

Body Folding: A **stress position** in which victims are seated on the ground with their legs touching in front of them. Their heads are bent down toward feet so the front half of their bodies are on their legs. The arms are tied behind their backs and lifted to a high wall. The head would be upside down in a ninety-degree angle. *How they get the body-folding victim mounted high on the wall upside down with the body still folded is not certain.* Origin: ancient China.

Boil: The act of putting people or parts of them in boiling water. See **alfet**. *Richard was boiled alive for poisoning the family he worked for as a private cook.* Origin: ancient Mesopotamian.

Bondage: To enslave a person either permanently or temporarily as an extreme form of community service or indentured servitude. Compare to **slavery**. *Bob was sentenced to heavy bondage for ten years.* Origin: ancient Mesopotamian.

Bone Breaking: The act of breaking nonlethal bones in the body as a harsh form of corporal punishment and usually done by specific tools for certain body parts. See **beating**. *Carlos broke several bones in Carla's arm for attempting to steal.* Origin: ancient Hebrew.

Body Suspension: To suspend a person in the air, sometimes with a **pulley** system, ropes, chains, claws, **iron collar**, **Spanish spider**, hooks, stakes for **impalement** or **picqueting**, **gibbet**, **Judas cradle**, or **hanging**. The person may be suspended from a wall or ceiling or even upside down. *Some people get multiple piercings in their back and practice body suspension with hooks on themselves just for fun.* Origin: ancient Hebrew.

Boo-Boo: See **little ease**.

Boot: See **iron boot**.

Boots: See **iron boot**.

Bootikins: See **iron boot**.

Bootkins: Scottish for **iron boot**.

Box: See **sweatbox**.

Branding: The act of taking a hot iron and applying it to people's skin to mark them for either a crime or to claim ownership over them as slaves. The letter "T" on the forehead meant thief, "V" vagabond, "B" blasphemer, "H" heretic, "A" adulterer/adulteress, "F" fornicator or someone who had had sex outside of marriage. "VRNK" was a thief or robber and punished by the **knout**. ("V" stood for *varnok*, which means settler or deportee.) Compare to **tattoo**, as both were used as punishment or to mark someone as a slave in both ancient Asia and ancient Europe, and the practices of both continued well into the Middle Ages. *It was common for thieves, vagabonds, and blasphemers to be branded on the chest or forehead.* Origin: ancient Hebrew.

Branks: A cage-like helmet in which scolds, liars, or blasphemers wore on scaffold as public humiliation. Inside the helmet is a very small pair of tongs that would hold a person's tongue stretched outward. Some branks have a mesh covering with a hole in the top so bees or other unpleasant insects or things could be poured in. Branks can come in a variety of styles. Compare with **iron gag** and **mask of shame**. *Wearing a pair of branks for too long can cause your tongue to swell, and you can choke to death on it.* Origin: Spanish Inquisition.

Brass Knuckles: Four metal rings connected by a metal piece held by the fist and the fingers inside the rings. Used for enhancing punches. *Brass knuckles used to be standard police equipment a long time ago.* The brass knuckles are a descendant of the ancient Greek **cestus**, a battle glove that was a gauntlet that sometimes had pieces of metal sticking out of it. This is also related to the Japanese **tekko**.

Brass Knucks: See **brass knuckles**.

Brass Monkeys: Canadian nickname for **brass knuckles**.

Brazen Bull: A hollow bull statue made of brass. Victims were placed inside and then burnt with a bonfire underneath the bull's stomach. Inside were tubes that pushed the victims' screams through the nostrils to make it seem like a live bull. Another version of it resembles an elephant, and yet another resembles a horse. There are other versions that are made to resemble other animals or even men or women as alternatives to **iron maiden,** but they are ultimately the same device. The brazen horse may be a primitive version of the brazen bull since the idea of it was inspired by the Trojan horse. The brazen bull is not to be confused with **iron bull.** *Perillus cooked inside his own oven the brazen bull for Phalarus' entertainment to demonstrate how it worked.* Origin: ancient Greece.

Brazen Elephant: See **brazen bull**.

Brazen Horse: See **brazen bull**.

Brazen Woman: An incandescent bronze statue of a woman filled inside with red-hot coals. A man who had sex with a woman outside his caste, committed adultery, or committed any other sex-based crime was forced to put his penis inside an open hole in the groin that completely resembled the vagina. She would be made to pose in a *Kama Sutra*-style manner, and the man would be forced into a certain kneeling position to complete the act. He would be tied down to it and would burn to death. It is *not* related to the **brazen bull** or the **iron maiden.** *Rajesh was sentenced to having intercourse with the brazen woman until he died because he had had sex with a widow.* Origin: ancient India.

Brazier: See **alfet**.

Breaking Wheel: See **wheel**.

Breast Ripper: A pair of four-pronged tongs, similar in look to ice pick tongs, that were designed to remove breast tissue by clamping tightly over the breast, turning, and then pulling, causing the breast to be ripped or broken off. The breast ripper was often heated or frozen for use. Compare to **wall of nails** and **spider** as these also removed breast tissue, although in a completely different manner (by shredding). Alternatively the breast ripper was also used to squeeze breast until pulverized or to mark the woman for a crime such as having children out of wedlock or adultery. *Thanks to the breast ripper, Lizzy Jane's ample breasts went from a double D to an A cup before death!* Origin: medieval Germany.

Bridal Bed: See **bed of nails**.

Bridport Dagger: Another name for a **noose**.

Brodequins: French for **iron boot**.

Bull Whip: A type of **stock whip** with an eight- to twelve-inch handle and a braided lash three to twenty feet long. The grip is wooden and sometimes exposed; however, the braid may cover it. The braids are made of leather. Not to be confused with **bullock-whip**. *As the name implies, bull whips were used to herd bulls.* Origin: ancient Roman.

Bullock-whip: A type of **stock whip** consisting of an eight- to ten-inch or longer lash made of green hide and a long handle cut from spotted gum or another tree. The handle was supposed to be taller than the user's shoulder. Not to be mistaken for **bull whip**. *A bullock team driver who uses a bullock-whip is called a bullocky.* Origin: modern Australia.

Buried Alive: The act of burying people, sometimes after they are forced to dig their own graves, and then covering them with the dirt they dug up so they would suffocate underground. *Sometimes when people were buried alive, their heads would be exposed. Instead of suffocating, they died of exposure, and people could watch them die.* Origin: ancient Roman.

Buried Alive Upside Down: See **tsirushi**.

Burning: 1. The act of setting people on fire and allowing the flames to consume them, melting them until they are only ashes. *Spanish Inquisitors were huge fans of burning heretics at the stake.* 2. Burning internally, the act of force-feeding or pouring molten lead or boiling pitch down the victims' throat with an iron ladle. *Mario was burned internally by being force-fed molten lead.* 3. The act of burning someone internally by putting a red-hot spit up the victim's anus or the act of disemboweling a person and replacing his or her entrails with hot coals. *Isabella ordered Edward to be burned internally with a red-hot poker up his rectum because he was gay.* 4. The act of making people walk on hot coals with their bare feet until death. *Fox dared the wimp to walk on hot coals, burning his feet.* 5. To put a flaming stick up people's noses so they have their sinuses burned and they suffocate on the smoke. *The kidnappers burned the children by putting flaming sticks up their noses because they wouldn't stop crying.* Origin: ancient Hebrew.

Burning Paper: Putting pieces of burning paper in between fingers and toes and then lighting them on fire. *Victims of the burning paper torture can suffer second-degree burns on the most delicate parts of their hands and feet.* Origin: ancient China.

Buskin: Another Scottish name for **Iron Boot**.

C

Cambuk: A wooden rod used to beat people. *The Cambuk was used to punish Indonesian slaves who were eventually shipped to South African slave owners. The whip went with them, and the South Africans pronounced it Sjambok.* Origin is ancient Indonesia, and the name comes from the ancient Persian **chabouk** or **chabuk**.

Camisole: Nickname for **straitjacket**.

Camisole de Force: French for **straitjacket**.

Caning: To whip or flog someone with a cane. See **bastinado**. *The vandal Kane was caned; he could not pay the fine for his crime.* Origin: ancient China.

Cannibalism: The act of eating a person alive as execution. Killing or cooking the victim first was optional. *Sometimes an adulterous couple was forced to eat each other until one of them died, but the one left alive would be forced to continue the cannibalism by eating the corpse until they died.* Origin: Ancient Nigeria.

Canshixing: Chinese for "offender's reproductive organs removed" for both male and female.

Capital Punishment: The act of executing a person, the act of putting a person to death for a serious crime. Compare to **corporal**

punishment. *The murderer was sentenced to capital punishment in the electric chair.* Origin: ancient Hebrew.

Capucha: Spanish for "rubber hood," which was used for **hooding** and **suffocation**.

Carding: To scratch or gouge a person using either red-hot iron combs or a **cat's paw**. *Saint Blaise's seven girlfriends collected drops of his blood while he was carded with red-hot combs. After he was beheaded, all seven girls were put in iron chairs and burned with a fire underneath of them until they all died.* Origin: ancient Rome.

Cask of Amontillado: A hollow crevice or niche a person is put inside. Then a wall is constructed to trap the person inside as a form of **burying alive** or **immurement**, and the person then starves to death. A cask of Amontillado can also be a room or series of rooms a person is locked away in, and the person can starve to death, never to be seen again. *Fortunado bricked Amontillado into a wall, and it became his cask, as he was buried and he starved to death.* Origin: medieval Italy.

Castaway: A person who is abandoned, **marooned**, or **exiled** to a remote location, usually a deserted island. *The word castaway can also refer to a person who is shipwrecked on a deserted island by accident.* The punishment of being exiled originates in ancient Mesopotamia; the word *castaway* originates in medieval England.

Castration: The act of removing the entirety of a person's genitals with a pair of sharp blades or a single blade such as a sword, ax, guillotine, or similar tool. Partial castration is cutting off one or both of a man's testes or the removal of fallopian tubes or ovaries in a woman. See **circumcision**. *The rapist was rightfully castrated.* Origin: ancient Mesopotamian.

Castrator: 1. A blade or pair of blades designed to castrate male or outside female genitalia. 2. The Italian word for **crocodile shears**. *The Armenian dwarf's favorite tool was the castrator.* Origin: ancient Roman.

Cat: Short for **cat o' nine tails.**

Catapelta: The act of sandwiching a victim between two boards and then adding weight so the victim is crushed. *The criminal was the key ingredient in a catapelta sandwich.* Catapelta is the Spanish word for **peine forte et dure**, which is the French term. The French did not necessarily make the victim lay between two boards, but they had the victim on the ground with the body-length board and stones on top of him or her. Putting the victim in a board sandwich was a Spanish idea, but it is virtually the same execution method. The first mention of any version of this execution refers to ancient Rome.

Catherine Wheel: Another word for the **wheel**, named for famous victim St. Catherine of Alexandria in ancient Roman times.

Cat o' Nine Tails: A type of heavy, two-handed whip with nine chains and/or straps with pieces of sharp metal on the ends, used to beat or whip someone to death or as extreme corporal punishment. *The mutineer pirate was whipped to death with the cat o' nine tails.* Origin: ancient Roman.

Cattle-Driving Whip: See **drafting whip.**

Cattle Prod: A metal bar accompanied with pincers used to electrocute someone by pushing a button on the handle. *The cattle prod, as the name implies, was originally used to herd cattle.* Origin: modern southern United States.

Cat Torture: 1. See **cauldron** definition two, as sometimes they used cats instead of rats. 2. To put an otherwise naked person into oversized pants or a sack and put a cat inside. Then to beat or suffocate the animal so it bites and scratches the victim viciously. It is also related to tying one in a sack full of animals. *Like the cauldron, cat torture is a form of animal cruelty.* Origin: ancient Roman.

Cat's Paw: A pair of metal claws worn over the knuckles that sometimes has metal pieces extended over the wrist. It can be a weapon in close-range combat as well as a torture device when the claws are heated or frozen. *The huntress' favorite weapon was the cat's paws she wore with her jungle cat costume.* Origin: Spanish Inquisition.

Cauldron: 1. See **alfet**. 2. A small, metal kettle big enough to house rats, cats, small dogs, or ants placed upside down over the victim's stomach, with the animals inside and a fire on the bottom of the kettle, pushing the animals to disembowel the victim by digging a tunnel through them to escape the intense heat. *The cauldron was a form of animal cruelty. Just imagine what the poor small animals had to go through trapped like that and forced to dig their way out through entrails full of feces.* Origin: ancient Roman.

Cavalry: See **Golgotha**.

Cave of Roses: A cave filled with poisonous reptiles and insects in which one or more victims was put in so they would be bit and stung to death. Another version was to just fill a well-lit room or a dark room with poisonous reptiles and insects so the victims could watch themselves die. *The term* roses *in* cave of roses *is a metaphor for the poisonous reptiles and insects.* Origin: medieval Sweden.

Cement Shoes: A person's feet are put in cinder blacks, and then they are filled with wet cement. The cement is allowed to harden and dry, and then the person is thrown into a body of water to drown. *When people are wearing cement shoes, they cannot use their legs to swim, and the weight of the cement makes them sink to the bottom. That's where their drowned remains will be.* Origin: modern United States.

Cestus: A battle glove made of leather or metal straps that may or may not have metal spikes decorating it. *Gladiators in ancient Rome would wear cestuses and beat one another to death in the arena.* Origin: ancient Greece.

Chabouk: A wooden rod used to beat people. *The Chabouk eventually made its way to Indonesia, and they called it Cambuk, their closest translation. Later it made its way to South Africa, where the slave masters called it Sjambok.* Origin: ancient Persia.

Chabuk: Alternate spelling of **chabouk.**

Chain Gang: Multiple pairs of handcuffs, manacles, belly chains, and sometimes heavy metal balls designed to organize and restrict two or several miscreants at once, normally only practiced when there are more prisoners than guards so they are easier to handle. Usually the prisoners would perform community service in public, and the chain gangs were designed to prevent them from escaping. *Chain gangs often inspire the chained miscreants to work together to escape. Consequently chain gangs are not really reliable.* Origin: modern southern United States.

Chain Whip: A short, one-handed whip with three or more chains that each have multiple segments of seven links and accompanied by flags for visual appeal, stability, and control, creating a whooshing sound in the air as it is used to beat or whip a person or to defeat an enemy in close combat. It was originally used in Chinese martial arts of multiple disciplines. *After he was publicly beaten with a chain whip, the pickpocket vowed never to pickpocket again.* Origin: ancient Chinese.

Chair of Nails: A metal armchair with 1,500 to two thousand metal spikes covering all the areas a person would use to sit, such as buttocks, back, shoulders, calves, forearms, and feet, plus restraints for the legs and wrists used for interrogation purposes or execution to bleed a person to death. It could also be heated, causing additional pain. *The* executioner sat on the victim's lap to restrain and press him further into the *chair of nails.* Origin: Spanish Inquisition.

Charlot: Nickname for an executioner. *Monsieur Charlot put the last king and queen of France to death.* Origin: French Revolution, originated with Charles-Henri Sanson, a famous French executioner.

Chastity Belt: Metal underwear covering the genitals of the wearer with a plate of spikes so that he or she cannot have sexual intercourse without the lover (or rapist) hurting themselves. There are several versions of chastity belts and sometimes they were very decorative. The Florentine girdle or **partial pudenda** only covered the vagina whereas the girdle of Venus, girdle of purity, or **full pudenda** also covered the buttocks and had holes surrounded by close-knit spikes for urinating and defecating. All chastity belts have a lock and key, so the wearers cannot take them off and commit adultery. Alternatively, some women chose to wear chastity belts to avoid being raped. *Aphrodite used olive oil to slip out of her chastity belt so she could continue her affair with Ares.* Origin: ancient Greece.

Che lie: Chinese for "**beheading** and **quartering**" or "torn apart by chariots and then beheaded."

Chelsea Grin: See **Glasgow smile**.

Chelsea Smile: See **Glasgow smile**.

Cheval de Bois: French for "**Spanish donkey**," literally translated as "horse of wood" or "**wooden horse**."

Chi: A whipping by a bamboo stick, cane, or clapper ten, twenty, thirty, forty, or fifty times depending on the degree of the crime. This was on some of the lists of the Chinese **five punishments**. *The runaway slave was sentenced to Chi and humiliation.* Origin: ancient Chinese.

Chicotte: Portuguese for **whip**. *In Portuguese African colonies and the Congo Free State, chicotte refers to a Sjambok with nails added to the lash.* The word *chicotte* is Portuguese for a generic leather whip. The Sjambok is South African.

Chinese Iron Maiden: A humanoid-shaped coffin that is completely hollow inside but has a grated bottom so hot coals underneath can steam the victim alive. There are no spikes inside unlike the Greek **iron maiden**. *Mushi was steamed like a vegetable in the Chinese iron maiden.* Origin: ancient Chinese.

Chinese Sunburn: See **Indian sunburn**.

Chinese Water Torture: To tie a person down to a table so they cannot move and pour continuous streams or drops of water on their head. Over time, the drops or streams will seem to get heavier and after a very long time, the person's skull will be exposed. See **waterboarding**. *Victims who survive the Chinese water torture are often insane because of it.* Origin: ancient Chinese.

Choke Pear: See **pear of anguish**.

Choking: The act of making a person's windpipes collapse by crushing the neck. See **strangulation, hanging**, and **garrote**. *The misogynist choked his wife to death.* Origin: ancient Hebrew.

Chopping Block: A chunk of wood over which a person's body part is stretched and is tied down to. It is used as a prelude to beheading by **ax**. *Without the chopping block, it is difficult to decapitate someone with an ax.* Origin: ancient Hebrew.

Chou-Da: To whip a person with a cane with its end split into many sticks. The punisher's goal is to rupture all internal organs without leaving a mark or bruise on the skin. *Executioner Fung had to learn to* *chou-da a pudding without breaking its surface before he first practiced it on a person.* Origin: ancient Chinese.

Cicogna: Italian for *stork*, this is their name for scavenger's daughter.

Cisi: The Chinese word for **hara-kiri**, translated literally as "permission to commit suicide." The choices of suicide may have ranged from hara-kiri to poison or throat slitting.

Cilice: 1. A coat of sharp goat hair or quills pointed inward to cause skin irritation. Modern versions made of metal have 612 spikes pointed inward. Some cilices, both metal and cloth, have the goat hair or spikes pointed outward to show penance rather than to feel it. Some have spikes pointed both outward and inward. Compare to **curaisse**. It is also called a hair shirt or sackcloth. 2. A spiked chain worn around the right thigh is also called a cilice because it's worn for the same purpose. A longer chain could also be squeezed tightly around the waist or upper bicep. *The monk wore a cilice for several days and nights as part of his penance.* The word *cilice* is Italian, coming from the Latin word *cilicia*, but the ancient Hebrews invented the first sackcloth or hair shirt.

Circumcision: The removal of foreskin in male victims or entire removal of clitoris, pubic mound, labials, the sewing shut of vaginal opening and vulva in female victims. In ancient cultures in which male circumcision was not practiced on male infants eight days old for religious and/or cleanliness reasons, adult male sex offenders were publicly circumcised by mutilation shears as a warning not to commit the same crime again or be castrated. Strict Muslim and Sikh sects have practiced female circumcision on young girls aged anywhere from newborn to sixteen years old (depending on region in Middle East or Africa or religious or cultural sect) for centuries, but ancient China used female circumcision and castration on adult women who committed adultery or abortion. The only difference between female circumcision and female castration is that female castration also removes the uterus in a Caesarean-style manner, and the victim is either left to die or be strangled or hanged by it. There are four categories of female circumcision. Type one is the removal of the clitoris and the clitoral hood that surrounds it. Type two is the removal of the clitoris, clitoral hood, and the smaller section of the labials that is closest to the vaginal opening. Type three is the removal of the clitoris, clitoral hood, all sections of the labials, all external genitalia. A stick or rock salt is put inside the vaginal opening. After this the girls' legs are bound tightly from hip to ankle and kept this way for fifteen to forty days. During this time the labial tissue binds itself across the vulva as it heals, except for the stick or salt that leaves a small hole for urination or agonizing sexual intercourse. The idea was that if sex was that painful, the girl wouldn't commit adultery. Type four is quite simply an umbrella for any other surgery, piercing, pricking, stretching, implantations, reversing of female circumcision, burning, branding, cauterization, or any other procedure that harms the vagina that isn't categorized by the first three types. A girl who endures type-three procedures may on a later date see a doctor to get her vaginal opening enlarged or reconstructed based on what her vagina might have looked like. Women in Western cultures who gets their clitoral hoods or labials pierced or undergo plastic surgery subject themselves to type-four circumcision. *Young Rania died of an infection after he was circumcised.* Origin: ancient Hebrew.

Circus: See **arena**.

Clamp: A cuff that is designed to restrict a body part that is not the wrists or ankles. The shape of the cuff is determined by what body part it is designed to restrain. Most are ring-shaped and adjustable, but some can be square or any other shape. *There is no body part in the human anatomy that cannot be restricted by a clamp of some sort.* Origin: ancient Mesopotamia.

Clapper: A popsicle-shaped bamboo wand with three bamboo lashes at the ends. The lashes are stiff and broad, and one is sandwiched in between the other two. This is a Lesser-known short **whip**. When it hits something, one of the side lashes smacks into the center one and reverberates the end one. The result is a loud clapping sound, hence, the name. *The clapper is one of the loudest short whips.* Origin: ancient China.

Clink: A nickname for a prison originating from the clinking noises of chains. *The first prison to be called the clink was Southwark Prison in England.* Origin: medieval England.

Club: A blunt wooden instrument used to flog a person as either corporal or capital punishment. Some clubs have spikes on them. If they are on fire, then they're called **torches**. Compare to **cudgel**. *The prostitute was flogged by a club and then buried alive.* Origin: ancient Mesopotamian.

Cnotta: Anglo-Saxon for **knout**. It later became the English word *knot*, so the Anglo-Saxon version of the knout was similar to the ancient Swedish **knut piska**.

Coat of Shame: See **barrel pillory**.

Cold Cell: See **hypothermia**.

Colombian Necktie: The act of slitting the person's throat, killing him or her instantly, but then reaching through wound to pull the person's tongue out for effect, making it so the tongue appears to be a bloody necktie from a distance. *The Colombian drug cartel used the Colombian necktie to intimidate rival gangbangers.* Medieval England practiced the slitting of the throat and pulling out the tongue on pirates as a sanctioned execution long before the gangs of modern-day Colombia did.

Community Service: To make a person a servant for the public or for a family, company, or organization without payment as a punishment.

The starlet was made to perform community service for her actions. Origin: ancient Chinese, see **tu**.

Controlled Fear: See **threat**.

Conveyor: A form of sleep deprivation in which more than one interrogator take shifts, keeping one prisoner awake and questioning or punishing the person. *The interrogators came one after another as though they were on a conveyor belt that led to that dark room.* Origin: Soviet Russia.

Copper Boot: See **iron boot**.

Coprophagia: The coercing or forcing a person to eat feces. Compare to **urophagia** and **menstrualphagia**. *Hank put feces in Mac's hot chocolate and asked him to drink it while Herbert put a gun to his head.* Origin: ancient Mesopotamia.

Corporal Punishment: The act of disciplining someone for a crime or misdemeanor in a nonlethal manner. Compare to **capital punishment**. *The prankster was handled with corporal punishment.* Origin: ancient Hebrew.

Cracker: Another name for the **lash**.

Cramp Word: A death sentence. *The judge uttered cramp words.* The death sentence has always been used as an execution ever since ancient Mesopotamian times. The phrase "cramp words" was coined in medieval England.

Crapping Cull: Another word for **hangman**. *The crapping cull crapped some hangings.* Medieval Netherlands comes from Old Dutch *crappen*, meaning "to snap," which described the hanging victim's neck if he or she was hanged right.

Crime: An illegal act or offense committed by one or more people against other people, offenses that are serious enough for the criminal(s) to deserve punishment for that crime. *Thousands of crimes are committed across the world every day.* The etymology of the word *crime* originates in ancient Latin, meaning *judgment* or *offense*, derived from another word that means "to judge." Crimes have been in existence since the dawn of humanity in ancient Mesopotamia.

Criminal: A person who commits a crime and deserves punishment for that crime, especially a serious one. *If criminals weren't punished for their crimes, society would descend into anarchy and chaos.* The word *criminal* originates in medieval England. Criminals have been in existence since the dawn of humanity in ancient Mesopotamia.

Crocodile Shear: A pair of shears with tubes inside lined with many spikes. Sometimes they are heated or frozen, or they have no treatment at all. They were used against those who attempted or succeeded in committing regicide. *Crocodile shears were also used for opera singers to commit autocastration to maintain a high, glass-shattering voice or by men who wanted a sex change.* Origin is Italian, but the Italians call it "Il **castrator**" while the English call it crocodile shears because they are shears and the spiked tubes are as sharp as crocodile teeth.

Crocodile Tube: A long metal tube filled with spikes that could fit a person's entire body with only the head and feet exposed at each end. The tube would be heated, and the person would burn to death. *Another version of this was a smaller tube still lined with spikes that could only fit an arm or leg; however, it crushed the limb inside like a vise, and heating it made it more painful.* Origin: Spanish Inquisition.

Crook: 1. Another word for **scourge**. 2. Another word for **criminal**.

Crop: See **riding crop**.

Cropping: The act of taking a metal cone, filling it with hot tar or pitch, then placing it on a person's head like a hat, allowing it to cool and then ripping it off. This severe form of **scalping** may expose the skull. A person who is a victim of this or a person who is bald on top with hair on the sides and back of the head is called a croppy, as it would appear that he was victimized in this way since the pitch takes off the hair on top. Because of these things, rebels were often nicknamed croppies, and cropping was the prescribed punishment for them. *Ian the Croppy wore a hot hat once, and when he took it off, he got a new haircut and a hot head. He was a cropping victim.* The English invented this torture in Ireland during an ancient Irish-English war a millennia ago. Only the Irish were documented to have been victimized by this.

Crown of Thorns: Thorns from plants (or barbed wire) that are interwoven into a circle and are then placed around a person's head just above the eyes. The thorns dig at the skull and eventually may break through to the person's brain. *Christ wore a crown of thorns as a part of his torture before execution.* This originated in ancient Greece. The crown of thorns came from the idea of athletes and mythological figures wearing wreaths around their heads. The crown of thorns was also the precursor to the **skull splitter.**

Crucifixion: The act of nailing or tying a person to two beams shaped like the letter "t" and leaving the individual up there to suffocate or die of exposure. The first form of crucifixion was to hang the person's body on a tree. *To Christians, crucifixion is not only an execution method but a symbol of their religion.* Origin: ancient Greece.

Cruel Shoes: See **instep borer.**

Crushing: The act of putting intense weight on a person or body part, causing it to collapse and bones to break, sometimes causing death. Crushing can also be caused by sandwiching the person or body part between two pieces of metal or stone and bringing those two things together. Another way to crush people is to wrap them in skin or untanned leather and leave them in the sun, which causes the wrap to continuously shrink. **Burying a person alive** can sometimes crush the victim. See **peine forte et dure, hand crusher, head crusher, toe breaker,** and **catapelta**. *The heavy debris fell on him, and he was slowly crushed to death long before he could be rescued.* Origin: ancient Hebrew.

Cry Cockles: The sound victims make when they are being strangled or hanged, to be hanged. *The victim uttered a cry cockle as his last words.* Origin: medieval England.

Cucking Stool: See **ducking stool**.

Cudgel: A club-like weapon sometimes covered with spikes and used to beat a person as either corporal or capital punishment. Also the name of a stick used in primitive **garrottes** and **knotted rope.** Compare to **club**. *The prostitute was flogged by cudgels and then buried alive.* The word cudgel is ancient Roman, but the first club was used by the ancient Mesopotamians.

Cuff: 1. An adjustable, round metal or leather ring or band that is designed to restrict the movement of any body part. Particular cuffs are designed to restrict. 2. Another word for **Slap**. *The most common cuff is the handcuff.* Origin: ancient Mesopotamia.

Culla di Giuda: Italian for **Judas cradle**.

Curaisse: A suit of armor lined on the inside with spikes with the wearer restrained by three to four interlocking bands fastened tightly so he or she cannot sit or walk normally. The wearer can only walk with stiff knees, or the person may not walk at all if he or she does not want to be cut. Additional torture would be administered to make the person walk quickly or to push the wearer so that he or she falls and is impaled to death. *Kyle was made to walk across a river of hot coals while he* was wearing a heated *curaisse*, so he was both burned and impaled to death. The word *curaisse* is French for armor, but the device was invented in medieval Germany.

Cutting: The act of using a sharp tool to break open someone's skin and make the person bleed. See **thousand cuts** and **twenty-four cuts.** *Po bled to death from the endless cuttings.* Origin: ancient Chinese.

Cyphon: A pillory in which a milk- and honey-covered victim was left until he or she either starved to death, died of exposure, or was bitten and stung to death by insects. *Sometimes if cyphon victims survived for twenty days, they were taken out, dressed in drag, and then thrown off a cliff face-first by an angry mob.* The origin is ancient Greek. The cyphon was the precursor and inspiration of **scaphismus.**

Cyphonism: See **cyphon.**

D

Dagger: See knife.

Dance at the Sheriff's Ball and Loll His Tongue Out at the Company: To struggle while hanging and to have one's tongue sticking out at the same time. *The unattractive man danced at the sheriff's ball and lolled his tongue out at the company who watched him die.* Origin: medieval England.

Dance the Hempen Jig: To hang. *The dancer danced the hempen jig at the end of the rope.* Origin: medieval England.

Dance the Newgate Hornpipe: To struggle at the end of the rope when one is hanging. *The wench danced the Newgate hornpipe.* Origin: medieval England.

Dance with Jack Ketch: To hang. *Jack Ketch was the name of an infamous hangman in England, and this is where the phrase "to dance with Jack Ketch" comes from. The term Jack Ketch can be used to mean any executioner.* Origin: medieval England.

Da Pi: Chinese for "death sentence."

Dark Gardens: Another word for **Death Row**.

Davy Jones' Locker: Medieval British slang for the ocean floor, where medieval pirates went, as they were commonly executed by drowning.

After he walked the plank, the corsair fell and drowned in Davy Jones' locker. Origin: medieval England.

Deadly Nevergreen: A name for the gallows. *The felons hanging on it are nicknamed the fruit of the deadly nevergreen tree, which it bears all year round.* Origin: medieval England.

Deafness: To cause a person to go deaf either temporarily with **evil noise** or permanently by shoving a red-hot **poker** into the ear canal and putting out the eardrum, pouring hot wax into the ear canal, or putting insects like bees or ants in the ear in hopes that their bites or stings will put out the eardrum. *Too much evil noise can also cause permanent deafness.* Origin: ancient Mesopotamian.

Death Row: A room, suite, or prison that only houses prisoners awaiting execution. *Death row is constantly having people come and leave it. No one stays there for too long.* Origin: ancient Mesopotamian.

Decapitation: See **beheading**.

Dedovschina: Russian for **hazing**.

Dehydration: To deny prisoners any water so they die of thirst. *It takes about three days for an average person to die of dehydration.* Origin: ancient Mesopotamian.

Dempster: Scottish for **hangman**. *The Dempster killed a lot of miscreants and made the city of Glasgow a safer place to live.* Origin: medieval Scotland.

Denailing: The act of extracting one's fingernails and/or toenails, usually with a pair of pliers, the precursor of inserting nails or needles underneath the nail bed, otherwise known as **nail insertion**, which was optional. *The hand model's career ended when she was denailled.* Origin: ancient North America.

Derrick: 1. A name for a hangman. 2. Another name for the gallows. 3. Another name for a gibbet or gibbet-shaped crane. *Derek the derrick hanged some people and left the rest of his victims to die in gibbets.* Origin: medieval England.

Diele: A primitive decapitation device with two short uprights, a blade resting on the victim's neck, and a mallet bashing it in to decapitate the victim. *Pere Jean-Baptiste was inspired by John of Bavaria's diele so much that he created another beheading device that was the inspiration for the guillotine.* Origin is medieval Germany. *Diele* today can be the German word for hall, plank, vestibule hallway, foyer, batten, deal, floor, board, threshing floor, or a person's last name. The beheading device's name may have come from the two upright planks that supported the blade.

Discipline: To punish or rebuke a person for an offense. *The naughty girl was disciplined by her man.* Origin: ancient Mesopotamian.

Disembowelment: To cut open and remove or burn the internal organs. *Christian martyrs were frequently disemboweled.* Origin: ancient Roman.

Disembowelment Crank: A rod with a crank. The victims are made to lie down on their back under the rod, and their abdomens are slit. A hook is attached to the rod by chains or rope, and the hook is stuck deep into the person's abdomen and is hooked onto the beginning of the person's intestines. As the crank is turned, the intestines are pulled out and are then wrapped around the rod until all the intestines are gone from the person. *If it weren't for the disembowelment crank, we probably wouldn't know how long the intestines really were or how much they weighed.* Origin: ancient Roman.

Disembowelment Drill: A device resembling a ceiling fan with blades turned vertically and a large drill in the center. The victim is pinned on the ground, and mechanisms operate the drill and make the many blades of the fan spin in a helicopter-like style. It descends on the victim from the ceiling. The victim is usually laid in a way so the bowels are targeted. *Angelica watched as the disembowelment drill slowly descended from the ceiling.* Origin: medieval Germany.

Disfigure: The act of mutilating someone, particularly in the face and/or genitalia. Nonfatal places to mark the person for a crime are generally targeted. *A person could also be born with a defect that could mark him or her disfigured for life.* Origin: Ancient Byzantium.

Dismemberment: To cut off or pull apart a person's limbs. *The Christian martyr was dismembered.* Origin: ancient Roman.

Dog Quirt: See **quirt.**

Doomster: Another nickname for a **hangman.** *The doomster brought doom to all those who opposed the law.* Origin: medieval Scotland.

Donkey of Shame: See **Spanish donkey, ride the rail,** or **wooden horse.**

Double-Neck Violin: A **neck violin** that can hold two people by their necks and wrists in a way so that they are facing each other. *The two women continued their catfight while both were contained in the double-neck violin.* Origin: Spanish Inquisition.

Drafting Whip: A type of **stock whip** that is a two-foot-six-inch fiberglass cane or rod with a handgrip, knob, wrist strap, and twelve-inch-long flapper for a lash. *Drafting whips were used for herding pigs and cattle in the Middle Ages.* Origin: medieval England.

Drawer: A narrow, closet-like prison cell with no windows or light, a cement bed, a hole in the floor as a toilet, and usually accompanied by a massive rat and insect infestation because of poor sanitation. *Gloria died of various illnesses because she lived in a drawer.* Origin: modern Cuba.

Dressage: Comes from the French word for training. A dressage whip is a forty-three-inch **whip** with a hook attached to the lash. *The purpose for the hook at the end of the dressage is to hook onto gates so the hunter can open these at a distance and also to keep the hunting dogs and servants away from the horse the person is riding.* Origin: medieval France.

Drill: A hardware appliance one can alternatively use to break into people's skin by drilling nails into them as opposed to into a wall. *The handyman was an expert at using his drill as a torture device.* Origin: ancient Saudi Arabia.

Driving Whip: A **longe whip** with a twelve-inch lash. *The lash of the driving whip is longer than the longe whip.* Origin: medieval England.

Drowning: The acts of submerging one's face in liquid or a wet cloth and making the person inhale it until death. This is the most common method of **suffocation**. *The ducking stool was used to drown supposed witches.* Origin: ancient Mesopotamian.

Drunk Barrel: See **barrel pillory**.

Drunk Tank: 1. See **ducking stool**. 2. See **barrel pillory**.

Drunkard's Cloak: Another name for **barrel pillory**.

Dry Pan: A large frying pan to cook someone in until the person is reduced to ashes. *The girl had been warned by the maid to obey the inquisitor, or else she would burn in the dry pan with a gradual fire.* Origin: Spanish Inquisition.

Ducking Stool: An iron chair a person was tied down to and then dunked into water by a crane or pulley. The person was sometimes dunked repeatedly as corporal punishment, or they were dunked once and left underwater long enough to drown as capital punishment. *The witch was dunked in the ducking stool.* Origin: Spanish Inquisition.

Duke of Exeter's Daughter: British nickname for the **rack**.

Dungeon: A place where prisoners are kept, interrogated, tortured, and sometimes executed underground, usually in a castle. Compare to **prison**. *The prisoner was kept in the dungeon for a long time.* Origin: ancient Egyptian.

Dunk Tank: See **ducking stool**.

E

Ear Chopper: A helmet with holes cut out for the ears and rotating blades on top designed to slice off the outer ear. *Dumbo couldn't fly anymore when he wore the ear chopper and lost his ears.* Origin: Spanish Inquisition.

Eaten by Animals: To be tossed to animals, the most common being lions, tigers, bears, snakes, crocodiles, insects, poisonous creatures, etc., and to be eaten by them. Any animal that eats meat can be used. *The adulterous Nigerian couple was eaten by crocodiles.* Origin: ancient Roman.

Eel of Ass: An eel used for the purpose of sodomizing a person as punishment. This is a form of **rhaphanidosis**. *The eel of ass was not limited to openly homosexual men. Men who committed adultery with other women were also prescribed this.* Origin: ancient Greek.

Eiserne Jungfrau: Ancient Greek for **iron maiden**.

Electric Carpet: A mat or actual carpet through which an electric current can be run through with cords. People are forced to stand or walk on it barefoot or naked as they are shocked. The torture can last for many hours before the carpet has to be charged, and it can carry up to five hundred thousand volts. *American Freemasons invented the electric carpet to use in initiation ceremonies, but what year or where is yet unknown.* Origin: modern United States.

Electric Chair: A wooden chair with a metal helmet designed to administer high-voltage electric shock to the felon in hopes of killing him or her instantaneously. See **electric shock**. *William died of a massive electric shock in the electric chair.* Origin: modern United States.

Electrical Generator: A generator used to electrocute someone as corporal punishment or interrogation. *The Frenchman used the electrical generator on the Algerian so much he had limb spasms for the rest of his life.* Origin: modern France.

Electric Shock: The act of shocking someone with an electric shock tool like a **cattle prod**, using an **electric generator,** hooking electric wires to bra straps, or administering high-voltage electrocution with an **electric chair**. *Mistress Electra liked to administer electric shocks to people.* Origin: modern United States.

Elephant: A large mammal instantly recognizable by its trunk, tusks, ears, gray skin, and very large size. An elephant can weigh as much as nine tons and is indigenous to the African continent and Southeast Asia, and they are revered religiously in India. In ancient times these highly intelligent, self-aware, cognitive, and empathetic animals were trained and used to torture and execute criminals. A quick and easy execution would have been to simply step on the person's head, but ancient elephants were trained to use their leads or metal armored tusks to flay people, impale them, disembowel them, or cut them. The elephants used their trunks to administer flagellations. They could hang the person or restrain them, dismember them by using their tusks, drag them across their tusks, or drag them across the ground. A person could be quartered between four elephants or be tied to one elephant's legs by a rope and dragged to death after he or she endured severe dislocations. An elephant would also step on a person's limbs and crush him or her without killing the person. Elephants were trained to break a person on the **wheel** in ancient Rome and Carthage. Unlike most animals that are used in executions, elephants do not operate by instinct alone and have reasoning. A death by elephant is guaranteed to be extremely painful and humiliating, and the elephants were trained to inflict routines of torture when the elephant was commanded to do so. *Execution by elephant was more popular in Southeast Asia and Rome than it was in Africa.* Origin: ancient India.

Emasculation: To belittle a person, usually a man, based on gender. This can be psychological, or this can be a physical manifestation, such as **circumcision, castration,** or partial castration. *The misandrous lesbian loved to emasculate men.* Origin: ancient Mesopotamian.

Escalara: Spanish word for ladder as in the **ladder rack**.

Equueleus: Latin for "young horse," which was the ancient Roman name for the **rack**.

Eve Teasing: See **sexual harassment**.

Evil Noise: A loud sound at the highest pitch played continuously and meant to cause hearing damage/loss and disorientation. It is a modern interrogation technique and sometimes paired with other tortures. *Marshall couldn't listen to his favorite music anymore because the evil noise caused him to go deaf.* Origin is modern United States. The **bell collar** was a precursor before the machine that created the evil noise was invented.

Evisceration: Another word for **disembowelment**.

Execution: To put someone to death. *The king ordered the execution of the traitor.* Origin: ancient Mesopotamian.

Executioner: A person paid by the government to put someone to death. *The executioner executed the traitor.* Origin: ancient Mesopotamian.

Executioner of the High Works: Another nickname for an executioner. *The executioner of the high works executed criminals of the high works.* Origin: French Revolution.

Exile: 1. To ostracize a person. *Carrie was exiled by her peers.* 2. To maroon a person at a remote location. *Napoleon was exiled on an island.* 3. To ban a person from one's own country and birthplace. *Charles was exiled from England and since roamed the Netherlands.* Origin: ancient Mesopotamian.

Expose: The act of leaving a person naked out in the open to die, to tie a person to a bench or flagpole, to put a person in a **gibbet** or **hanging cage** and leave him or her there, to expose the person to the public in **Stockades** for an hour, or to bury a person alive while naked. One could also be exposed naked and tied to a tree in a swamp for the mosquitoes or other animals and insects to eat. *Miranda felt exposed and lonely as she was taken to the town square naked in the middle of winter and was then doused with cold water, beaten, and left to die.* Origin: ancient Mesopotamian.

Eyelid Removal: To use a sharp object to cut off the eyelids. After this happened, the victim would've been buried naked up to the chin or tied to the ground face up and then left to starve to death. They would've had their eyes burned by the sun as a sadistic form of **abacination** before the starvation. *After the scalping, Stupid Horse had his eyelid removed and was buried so as to face the sun and have his eyes cooked for the ants to eat.* Origin: ancient North America.

F

Fagging: Another word for **hazing**.

Fall: 1. To throw a person off a cliff or other really high place or otherwise cause a person to die by falling. *Aesop was caused to fall off a cliff for stealing from Apollo's temple.* 2. A piece of leather attached to the end of the body of a **whip**. *Some whips have falls; others have the lashes directly attached to the body.* First definition origin: ancient Roman. Second definition origin: ancient Egyptian.

Fall of the Leaf: A hanging in which the victim first stands on a hinged board on a balcony. *Patrick fell like a leaf from a tree during his hanging.* Origin: medieval Ireland.

Feeding the Fish: To be thrown into the ocean. *One may either feed the fish as an execution with a live body or with dead one, disposing of the body after a different execution.* Origin: ancient Mesopotamia.

Female Circumcision: See **circumcision**.

Female Genitalia Mutilation: See **circumcision**.

Fen Weilu: Chinese for **quartering**.

Fetal Position: A **stress position** that forces a person to squat or lie down curled up in a ball. It gets its name from the way fetuses are depicted in medical drawings and art. *Being in fetal position can be hard on the ears, and fetuses aren't normally in that position anyway.* Origin: ancient Greece.

Felon: Another word for **criminal**.

Fetter: A **Manacle** that is used exclusively for securing a person's ankles. *He was fettered in heavy chains.*

Figging: To sodomize a person by using a peeled piece of ginger root. *Figging was also used before butt plugs were invented.* Origin: ancient Greece.

Fimbo: Belgian Congo name for the **sjambok**.

Finger Stocks: A form of **stockade** that is small and butterfly-shaped and has eight holes. There are four holes in each wing. Each wing can open up, making each hole a semicircle. The victim's fingers are put into the holes and are usually locked behind his or her back. It is a form of restraint used in place of **handcuffs**. *The practice of using finger stocks never really caught on. Handcuffs became more popular.* Origin: Victorian England.

Fire: A chemical combustion that eats oxygen while at the same time giving off extreme heat, used commonly in many tortures, such as a **gridiron, iron chair,** or **dry pan**, and executions, such as burning at the **stake** or **tunica molesta**. Fire can either play a large or small part in the suffering of a person. It may be exploited as a torture or execution in and of itself simply by lighting someone on fire, especially in combination with gasoline or other chemicals or flammable substances or materials. Heating up any kind of metal with fire and then applying it to someone's skin is also torture. Fire can come in a variety of colors ranging from yellow/orange/red to blue/black to white depending on how much heat is applied or where it comes from. *Most religions believe that eternal damnation is a large lake of black fire and brimstone of a white hot intensity that is inescapable and somehow never completely* consumes the people and demons inside, leaving them to agonize forever. Origin: Mesopotamia.

Firing Squad: A group of executioners with guns, bows and arrows, darts, or crossbows gathered together to shoot one criminal to death. Sometimes the victim was put on a spinning wheel so as to make a game of what body part got hit or to test the marksmanship of the executioners. *In medieval times criminals were put to death by firing squads with bows and arrows or crossbows since guns weren't invented yet.* Origin: ancient Denmark.

Five Pains: To amputate the nose, one hand, one foot, and genitals (regardless of sex) and then cut in half across victim's waist, gutting the person. Compare to **twenty-four cuts** and **thousand cuts**. This is *not* related to **five punishments**. *The five pains is a simplistic variant of the twenty-four cuts and the thousand cuts.* Origin: ancient China.

Five Punishments: A list of punishments for criminals according to their different classes or crimes. The five punishments for slaves were (1) forehead tattoo with indelible ink, (2) nose cut off, (3) amputation of either or both feet and/or removal of both kneecaps, (4) castration for either male or female and for sex-related crimes such as adultery, licentiousness, and promiscuity, and (5) execution. The methods of execution varied from quartering, boiling alive, being torn apart by chariots, decapitation, strangulation, slicing process (see **thousand cuts**), or other methods. The body would be abandoned in the local market. The five punishments for serfs were (1) flagellation with a light bamboo cane or bamboo clappers of which there were five degree (ten, twenty, thirty, forty, or fifty lashes), (2) flagellation with a large stick of which there were also five degrees (sixty, seventy, eighty, ninety, or a hundred lashes), (3) penal servitude with five degrees (one year plus sixty strokes of the big stick, one and a half years plus seventy strokes, two years plus eighty strokes, two and a half years plus ninety strokes, three years plus a hundred strokes), (4) exile to a remote location and forbidden to return to birthplace of which there were three degrees

(620 miles plus a hundred strokes of the large stick, 775 miles plus a hundred strokes, 930 miles plus a hundred strokes), (5) death penalty. The only options were strangulation, decapitation, or slicing process along with decapitation. Any of these punishments could be remitted through payments made in copper cash, but the more severe the punishment, the higher the pay. The five punishments for female offenders were (1) being forced to grind grain, (2) fingers squeezed between sticks, (3) flagellation with wooden staves, (4) permission to commit suicide (see **hara-kiri**), (5) or sequestration or confinement to a room for licentiousness or adultery. *Emperor Song rewrote the lists of five punishments.* Origin: ancient Chinese.

Five Techniques: A list of interrogation techniques used by Northern Ireland and Great Britain. They are **wall-standing, hooding, evil noise, sleep deprivation, and starvation.** *Prisoners suffered any and all combinations of these five techniques.* Origin: modern United Kingdom.

Flagellation: To whip someone severely, usually killing the person. *You could kill someone with flagellation just by targeting the kidneys, causing them to fail.* Origin is ancient Hebrew. The word flagellation comes from the Latin word **flagellum**, which refers to the **scourge whip**.

Flagellum: Latin for **scourge**.

Flagrum: Another Latin word for **scourge**.

Flail: 1. A long rod with a chain lash with a metal ball covered in spikes at the end. 2. Another word for **scourge**. *The knight flailed his flail and knocked some people down.* Origin: first definition in ancient Roman, second in ancient Egyptian.

Flapper: A type of **lash** that consists of many short, firm, but flexible wires. *Flappers are most commonly seen at the ends of riding crops and other short whips.* Origin: medieval England.

Flay: The act of degloving skin off of the entire body piece by piece and leaving the person to bleed to death. *Jacopo and David were flayed alive by Waldenses who peeled them like large pieces of potatoes.* Origin: ancient Assyria.

Floating Prison: A ship used to contain prisoners, usually as a method of transport to and from different prisons across water. *Marysol was housed on the floating prison for weeks.* Origin: modern United States.

Flogger: A type of whip consisting of five or more leather straps and a string of beads made of either plastic or metal. *The beads are what make the flogger unique from other types of whips with the possible exception of the first cat o' nine tails.* Origin: medieval Italian, a descendent of the ancient Roman Cat o' Nine Tails and a relative to the Knout.

Flogging: See **flagellation**.

Florentine Girdle: A type of **chastity belt** that only covers the vagina. It is also called a **partial pudenda**. *Hephaestus made Aphrodite wear a Florentine girdle so she would stop having an affair with Ares.* Origin: ancient Greece.

Florida Cow Whip: A two-piece **stock whip** that is a twelve-foot lash connected to the handle by threading two strands of said lash through hollow part of wooden sixteen-inch handle before it's tied off. Both parts of the whip are made of cowhide, buckskin, or flat nylon parachute cord that can still be effective when wet. *Florida cow whips are sometimes still used by certain people today, but mostly for demonstration purposes and show.* Origin: modern United States.

Flute of Shame: See **noise-maker's fife**.

Flying Guillotine: A sack held open by a metal hoop at the opening and lined with a blade. On the other end of the sack is a string. The sack is placed over the person's head and completely covers it. The string is pulled, and the blade quickly cuts off the head and simultaneously closes the sack to carry the head. *The flying guillotine was used by ninjas to assassinate a person as quietly as possible.* Origin: ancient China.

Foot Press: A bar connected with an upper bar that is curved and on top of it is a crank. The foot is fixed between the bars, and the crank makes them press together to crush the foot. Sometimes there are rows of spikes embedded in the upper bar. This is called a **Venetian foot screw**. Also compare with **toe breaker**. *The foot press pressed Preston's foot like a Panini press.* Origin: Spanish Inquisition.

Foot Roasting: The act of putting a person in ankle stocks and then applying a hot iron to their feet as corporal punishment. Another method is to put hot coals under a person's feet and force the victim to walk on them. *The girl limped when she walked after her feet were roasted.* Origin: ancient Hebrew.

Foot Whipping: The act of putting people in ankle stocks and then whipping or caning the soles of their feet. See **bastinado**. *The boy limped when he walked after his feet where whipped.* Origin: ancient Hebrew.

Force-Feeding: The act of shoving food down one's throat but doing so carefully so that the person does not choke, feeding him or her until the stomach explodes. Then the person may be beaten and kicked to death. Another method was to first starve the person for days and then mash the tongue with a hammer or cut it deeply and then force-feed soup containing any or all of the following: lots of salt, lots of pepper, platypus poison, and/or acid. Alternately a victim may be obliged by torturers to eat and drink while he or she urinates and defecates at the same time. Bodily waste may be also used, such as **coprophagia**, **urophagia**, and **menstrualphagia**. Other inedible items such as sand or metal may be used or paper. Compare to **swedentrunk**. Force-feeding could also be a part of a bigger torture such as **scaphismus**. *The* *gluttonous lumberjack enjoyed being force-fed at first, but he soon realized that he had gotten more than he had bargained for.* Origin: ancient Mesopotamian.

Fry: To burn someone to death with oil or to bathe the person with lard and then apply hot pans filled with burning charcoal over various body parts until he or she dies. *Maccabeus and his family fried to death in a frying pan after they were dismembered and lost their tongues.* Origin: ancient Roman.

Full Pudenda: A type of **chastity belt** that covers the vagina and anus and has holes allowing for urination and defecation. The holes, however, are surrounded by spikes to prevent any kind of penetration or even foreplay or masturbation involving the clitoris or buttocks. This type of chastity belt is also called a girdle of purity or a girdle of Venus. *The young woman wore a full pudenda to avoid being raped.* Origin: ancient Greece.

Fustra: See **flagellation.** The word comes from the first definition of **fustuarium.**

Fustuarium: 1. See **flagellation.** 2. To cut down with a sword. 3. To put someone through a gauntlet or tournament of warriors, torturers, or other torments until the individual dies. *The banker was sentenced to fustuarium for usury.* Origin: ancient Roman.

Fuxing: Chinese for castration for either male or female because of adultery or any form of sexual immorality.

G

Gag: 1. A piece of material tied over or stuffed in a person's mouth for the purposes of making the person silent. 2. A rubber ball with a strap attached to it. The ball is inserted into the person's mouth, and the straps clasp around the other side of the person's head. It is designed for the purpose of making the person silent. 3. See **iron gag**. *The robbers gagged the woman to stop her from screaming.* Origin: ancient Mesopotamian.

Gag Pear: See **pear of anguish**.

Galga: The Saxon word for **gallows**.

Gallows: A tree or two wooden crossbeams shaped as a right angle on which one or more people would be hanged. *Medieval criminals were hanged on the gallows.* Origin: ancient Hebrew.

Gallows' Apple: A person being hanged. *The woman with the apple-shaped body hanged as a gallows' apple.* Origin: medieval England.

Gambler's Necklace: See **garrotte**.

Gaoler's Coach: A hangman's cart on which prisoners are transported from prison to scaffold. *The criminal had a one-way ticket to his death with a free ride on the gaoler's coach.* Origin: medieval England.

Garrotte: A chair with a metal wire or rope collar and a cudgel or lever used to tighten the collar to strangle the person. It was commonly used as an execution, but occasionally a person may be strapped into it and not strangled as a humiliation device. It is sometimes called a gambler's necklace. See **strangulation**. *The bookie was strangled to death in the garrotte after they laughed at him in it for two hours.* Origin is ancient India, but the word *garrotte* comes from the French word for cudgel.

Gas Chamber: A room filled with poisonous gas. The victim was locked inside and left to die. Sometimes the person would be confined to a chair while this took place, or the individual would bang on the door and beg to be released while he or she died. *The Holocaust prisoner banged on the locked door of the gas chamber as he lost his senses while the Nazi guards laughed at his futile attempts to escape.* Origin: modern United States.

Gauntlet: A tournament or arena where people were condemned to fight one another, other warriors, and torturers or endure other torments until death. Alternatively a gauntlet can also consist of several **club**-wielding men forming two parallel lines that prisoners run through and receive hits. *The gauntlet was a place for condemned prisoners to die like warriors, fighting to the death.* Origin: ancient Roman.

Gaveta: Spanish for **drawer**.

Gegene: French for "man-powered **electrical generator**."

Genital Mutilation: See **circumcision**.

Gentleman of the Three Ins: A person who was in prison, indicated, and due to be hanged in chains. *Leopold was a gentleman of the three ins as he was in prison, indicated, and about to be hanged alive in chains until death.* Origin: medieval England.

Gibbet: 1. A gallows. *The thief was hanged by the gibbet.* 2. A metal cage in which a person is placed naked and then left to die of starvation or exposure. See **hanging cage**. Origin: first definition Hebrew, second definition medieval England.

Glasgow Grin: See **Glasgow smile**.

Glasgow Smile: The act of cutting a person's face from the corners of their mouths to their ears so they look like they are smiling or grinning. Sometimes the person is then beaten to death, and the wounds are split open as they scream. Ironically it looks like they are laughing and enjoying it. *Duncan and his gang mugged people and left them smiling a Glasgow smile.* Origin: Victorian Scotland.

Golgotha: The name of the **scaffold** where Jesus Christ was crucified. The name means "place of the skull." **cavalry** was its Roman name. *The name of the modern subculture of Goth is derived from the name Golgotha, and skulls and other symbols of mortality are important to them because of it.* Origin: ancient Hebrew.

Gone West: Going in the direction of the route from prison to scaffold. *The prisoner went west in the hangman's cart from the tower to Tyburn.* Origin: medieval England.

Gong: Another Chinese word for castration for either male or female.

Gong-Xing: Chinese for **solitary confinement**.

Go to Rest in a Horse's Nightcap: To die in the noose. *The horse fetishist went to rest in a horse's nightcap after he was convicted of molesting one of the king's horses.* Origin: medieval England.

Go up a Ladder to Bed: To be hanged. *The sleepy prisoner went up a ladder to bed and went to sleep for eternity.* Origin: medieval England.

Great Knout: A **knout** with a twenty-four-inch handle with a flat leather strap twice as long, ending with a copper or brass ring attached to a hide two inches broad and ending in a point. *Rumor has it that Peter the Great may have murdered his son, Prince Alexis, with a great knout.* Origin: medieval Russia.

Gregorian Tree: The gallows. *Gregory the hangman hanged people on his Gregorian trees.* Origin: medieval England.

Gridiron: A large grill used to cook people until they died. *St. Lawrence died well-done on the gridiron.* Origin: ancient Roman.

Guillotine: A decapitation device consisting of a blade held upright by posts and secured by a rope. The victim would lie on a board with his or her head held fast in a neck stockade. Cutting the rope releases the blade and decapitates the person. *Dr. Joseph Guillotin based his invention, the guillotine, on ancient decapitation devices found throughout Europe.* Origin: French Revolution.

Gulag: A system of labor camps in which people die. *Ivan was imprisoned in a gulag.* Origin is Soviet Russia. The word literally means "death camp."

Gully: Medieval British slang for any knife or dagger.

Gunpowder: A flammable substance that can be used to cover a person's head or body. It can also be stuffed into orifices, such as mouth, vaginas, and/or anuses, and then set on fire, causing the victim to explode into microscopic pieces. *The protestant woman was tied between two trees, stuffed with gunpowder, and lit up. She exploded with a quick but messy and noisy death.* Origin: Ancient China.

H

Hair Pulling: To yank off hair from any body part. *Hair pulling does not require a special device, as anyone can do it with their fingers, but the scalping chair was made for scalping victims.* Origin: ancient China.

Hair Shirt: See **Cilice**.

Halifax Gibbet: A primitive beheading device in which a man laid on his back on the ground with his neck on a board. An ax blade was held far above and only supported by a rope. Severing the rope or having an animal or another person pull it would make the ax blade fall on the neck, severing the head. *Samuel was sentenced to beheading by Halifax gibbet under Halifax gibbet law for stealing cinnamon-flavored taffy.* Origin: medieval England.

Halsgiege: German for **neck violin**.

Haltering Place: The position of the **noose** knot that is under the left ear. *If the noose knot is not in the correct haltering place, the victim will only get a broken neck and won't die.* Origin: medieval England.

Hamstringing: To sever a person's heels where the hamstring muscle is so that the victim cannot walk. *The runner was forced into retirement because he was hamstrung by a jealous rival.* Origin: ancient Mesopotamian.

Handcuffs: A pair of metal rings that secure a person's wrists. *He was dragged before the court in handcuffs.* Origin: ancient Hebrew.

Hand of Glory: A hanged man's hand. *During the Middle Ages, a hand of glory was used as a charm or cure by practicing witches.* Origin: medieval England.

Hanging: The act of asphyxiating or strangling a person to death by holding the feet off the ground by the neck. *The thieves were hanged.* Origin: ancient Hebrew.

Hang Alive in Chains: The act of using several or more chains and gallows to suspend people above the ground and leaving them to die, similar in purpose to **gibbet** or **hanging cage**. *The Thames pirate was left to die by hanging alive in chains.* Origin: medieval England.

Hang Alive on a Tree: The earliest form of crucifixion was to nail a person to a tree and leave him or her to die. *The wicked priest was condemned to hang alive on a tree.* Origin: ancient Greece.

Hang at the Yard Arm: The act of hanging a person from a sturdy crosspiece mounted on the main mast of a ship. *The bad marine Private John was hanged at the yardarm for two attempted murders.* Origin: modern England.

Hang, Draw, and Quarter: The act of hanging a person for a minute or right before death—but then cutting them down, castrating them, disemboweling them, burning the severed body parts in front of them, beheading them, and cutting or pulling apart the rest of the body into four even pieces. *Traitors were hanged, drawn, and quartered.* Origin: medieval England.

Hanging Cage: A body-hugging cage in which a naked person is left to die of starvation or exposure. This person could also be covered in milk and honey and left to be bitten and stung by insects. Some hanging cages are made of wood, and when the person is inside, its set on fire and burns the victim. This is called a **wicker man**. Compare to **gibbet**. *Andrew was left to die in the hanging cage.* Origin: medieval England.

Hangman: An executioner who specializes in hanging people. *Jack Ketch was the worst hangman documented by history. It took several minutes for his victims to die.* Origin: ancient Hebrew.

Hangman's Day: Friday. *Hangings usually took place on Fridays, so Fridays were called Hangman's Day.* Origin: medieval England.

Hangman's Wage: The amount of money the government pays an executioner for a job, originally only applied to hanging. *In Medieval England and Scotland, a typical hangman's wage was thirteen and a half pence or one mark, which was enough to pay for the execution itself and the rope used to hang someone.* Origin: medieval England.

Hara-Kiri: Japanese for belly-cutting. It is a form of suicide characterized by self-disembowelment with a knife or a sword. *Taki was a disgraced nobleman who decided to commit suicide by using hara-kiri so that he wouldn't be hanged in public.* Origin: feudal Japan.

Have a Dry Mouth and a Pisson Pair of Breeches: The result of being hanged. The dry mouth comes from screaming or gasping for breath, and the "pisson pair of breeches" describes how a person's bladder and bowels automatically release upon death. *James had a dry mouth and a pisson pair of breeches from being hanged.* Origin: medieval England.

Hazel Rod: A bundle of four or five hazel twigs used to flog or whip people. *The hazel rod is the hazel tree equivalent of a birch rod.* Origin: medieval England.

Hazing: The act of beating, sexually assaulting, raping, or using psychological tortures such as pranking to accept a person as a new member of a college, military branch, gang, group, organization, class, or secret society. *Hazing happens because people generally don't like changes or meeting someone new, so the new person usually becomes an outcast or pet for pranks.* Origin: medieval Scotland.

Head Crusher: A metal helmet with a screw on top and a bar below the helmet. The victim's head was placed in between the helmet and bar. The screw either crushed the head slowly until death, or the helmet bashed into the head with repeated thrusts over and over until death. *After he was treated by the head crusher, the big man found he had a shrunken head.* Origin: Spanish Inquisition.

Hearty Choke: The typical last meal of a condemned hanging victim, an artichoke dipped in caper sauce. *The condemned man, who was a chef, thoroughly enjoyed the hearty choke he made for himself the night before his execution.* Origin: medieval England.

He'll Piss When He Can't Whistle: Refers to how one's bladder and bowels automatically release upon death and how one cannot whistle when they are being asphyxiated. *Kenny pissed when he couldn't whistle in the noose.* Origin: medieval England.

Hempen Casement: Another name for a **noose**. The word "hempen" refers to it being made of rope. Other names for it are hempen collar, cravat, habeas, and snare. *The hanging victim was naked save for the hempen casement.* Origin: medieval England.

Hempen Fever: To get hempen fever is to die by hanging. *Mary died of hempen fever.* Origin: medieval England.

Hempen Widow: A woman whose husband was hanged. *Elisabeth has been a hempen widow ever since Reginald was hanged.* Origin: medieval England.

Heretic's Fork: A choker necklace with a long, double-pronged fork in the center of the chain or strap designed to hold a victim's head up toward the sky and to stretch out the neck. One prong dug into the skin under the chin, and the other dug into the skin of the victim's clavicle right over the sternum. It was believed that in this position the victim couldn't pronounce or say correctly certain words, so he or she couldn't commit heresy, blaspheme, or use curse words. *While she was wearing the heretic's fork, Clumsy Callie couldn't look down to see where she was going, and she tripped and fell on her face a lot.* Origin: Spanish Inquisition.

Hitobashira: Japanese for human pillar. Women were burned alive at the base of construction sites as **human sacrifices** because it was believed that this would protect the buildings against natural disasters and enemy attacks. *The ancient Japanese condemned hundreds of women annually in the act of Hitobashira.* Origin: feudal Japan.

Hood of Shame: 1. See **mask of shame**. 2. See **hooding**.

Hooding: The act of wrapping a person's head with material or putting the head in a sack and tying it shut for the purposes of sensory deprivation or to hide the identity of the interrogator. It can cause disorientation, death by suffocation, and the inability to breathe properly. It is often used as a prelude to beating, interrogation, other tortures such as **evil noise** and **waterboarding**, and other execution methods such as **hanging** and **firing squad.** *Mustafa died in prison hooded the whole time.* Origin is ancient Hebrew. Hooding was originally used as a precursor to hangings and wasn't exploited as a torture in of itself until modern times. That originally started in Iraq but has since been used by all countries regardless of laws against it.

Horse: Prussian variant of **Judas cradle**, which was meant to inflict pain on male genitalia without breaking the skin. *Medieval Prussian soldiers who didn't follow orders or deserted a battle were disciplined by riding the horse.* Origin: medieval Prussia.

Horse Quirt: See **quirt**.

Horse Whip: A form of **riding crop**.

Horsing: To hold a miscreant by the arms on the back of another person or across the shoulders of several people depending on how tall the person is. This is done to hold the person still while he or she is being flogged. *When you are horsing someone, the person whipping the miscreant must be careful not to hit the people holding the victim in place.* Origin: medieval England.

Hot Box: A wooden box attached to the ground outside where a naked person is left in the intense heat. The person may be left to die, or after a few hours or days, the individual may be taken out and, if unconscious, revived by cold water. There is a slight possibility the person will go into shock. It is basically a combination of the **sweatbox** and the **little ease** box. *Hilda was left outside in the hot box for breaking eggs.* Origin: modern United States.

Hot Squat: Another name for an electric chair. *William fried in the hot squat.* Origin: modern United States.

Human Branding: The act of branding a victim, usually on the forehead, hand, or forearm to mark the person for a crime. To mark someone with a "T" on the forehead or hand would signify a thief. To mark someone with a "V" on the forehead would signify a vagabond. To mark someone with an "H" on the forehead would signify a heretic. To mark someone with a "P" on the wrist or forearm would signify a pirate. "VRNK" on the forehead stood for "settler/ deportee, thief, robber, and punished by the knout." The "V" stood for *varnok*, which meant either settler or deportee. Compare to **tattoo**. *After suffering through human branding like cattle, the victim usually either kills himself or only carries out his deeds at night.* Origin: ancient Mesopotamian.

Human Press: 1. See **catapelta** or **peine forte et dure**. 2. To sandwich people between two stretchers and sit on them. *The prison guard proudly took pictures of himself sitting on a homemade human press.* Human presses of all kinds have been around since ancient Rome.

Human Sacrifice: The act of killing a person or group of people in the name of religion. The act of sacrifice itself may include heart removal, burning, forced suicide by drinking poison, drowning, impalement, fighting another to death, hanging, buried alive, throat slitting, strangulation, bludgeoning on the head, dismemberment, stabbing, cannibalism, starvation, being shot by arrows, and flaying alive. This is not reserved for criminals only. Prisoners of war are always sacrificed first before random people. *The human sacrifice victim watched his still-beating heart burn just before he bled to death.* Origin is ancient Canaan, but this has since been practiced to some extent by most ancient cultures around the world with the exceptions of the religions Judaism, Christianity, and Islam.

Human Toilet: To tie naked people to chairs and then to urinate and defecate on them as though they were the receptacle or toilet. *The woman was used as a human toilet by several other men and women for days and eventually died.* Modern North Americans do this to Middle Eastern prisoners.

Human Urinal: Same as **human toilet**.

Humiliation: To shame or put down someone. **Public humiliation** is characterized by laughter, mockery, and throwing things at the person such as rotten food and fecal matter. Humiliation in private is usually characterized by the same treatment plus nonconsensual sexual assault and/or rape. Another way to humiliate people is to oblige them to drink a lot of water and then deny them a toilet, forcing them to soil themselves. *The outcast committed suicide after weeks of humiliation.* Origin: ancient Mesopotamia.

Hunting Crop: A **crop** with a stiff stock. One end has a seven-foot long lash, and the other end has a hook. *The boy used a hunting crop to protect his pet dog from wild pariah dogs.* Origin: ancient India.

Hypothermia: To put an exposed or naked person in an overly cooled room or a walk-in freezer. Alternatively the victim can be made to stand barefoot on snow while he or she holds a block of ice. The person can be sodomized by icicles or be tied to a tree outside when it is snowing. The freezer method is essentially the opposite of a **sweatbox**. *Jack died of hypothermia after he spent days in the freezer.*

I

Imbuvu: Zulu dialect for hippopotamus, which is their name for the **sjambok**, because it was most commonly made from hippopotamus hides.

Immurement: To be left outside in a box or crate or to be **buried alive**. It is related to **scaphismus** and **cyphon** in that the person lives out the rest of his or her days in a container, but there is no effort to increase insect activity. It is also similar to Chinese **stockades**. The **hot box** can also be considered a form of immurement if the person inside is left to die of heat stroke or **starvation**. *Immurement is still practiced in some Asian places today.* Origin: ancient China.

Impale: 1. The act of skewering a human body, whether it be in the stomach, chest, genitalia, anus, or mouth, sometimes involving more than one stake. A person could be thrown into a pit full of stakes. *Vlad's favorite execution was to impale the victim from anus to mouth with a long stake.* 2. See **iron maiden**. Origin: first definition ancient Egyptian, second definition ancient Greece.

Indian Sunburn: To twist a person's forearms until the skin is red. A more severe form of this torture would be to twist until the person's arms are sprained or broken. *Stupid Horse was given the Indian sunburn for his foolishness.* Origin: ancient Indian.

Inquisitor: Medieval term for a **questioner** or **torturer**.

Instep Borer: A metal boot with a knife blade inside with the handle sticking out from it. The torturer turned the handle or made thrusting motions with it so as to cut the sole of the person's foot. Instep borers could alternatively be made to resemble any other style of shoe, and variants can have spikes that impale people when they walk or rest their feet on the ground. *There is no evidence to suggest that instep borers were also made to tighten around the person's leg, making them a form of the iron boot.* Origin: Spanish Inquisition.

Interrogation: To question a person for the sake of solving a crime and to best decide how to proceed in an investigation. Interrogation can be enhanced with torture or the threat thereof. A long period of interrogation is a form of **sleep deprivation**. *The suspect was interrogated for two days straight by several police men who took turns.* Origin: ancient Mesopotamian.

Interrogation Chair: See **chair of nails**.

Intestinal Crank: See **disembowelment crank**.

Iron Apega: See **iron maiden**.

Iron Bed: 1. See **bed of nails**. 2. See **gridiron**.

Iron Boot: A pair of metal boots meant to tighten around the victims' legs until totally pulverized. A more primitive version was to nail boards around a victim's legs and then pound them with a hammer or mallet until the shin bone shattered. Another method was to wrap the leg in a cloth and tighten it as much as possible and then allow shrinking in the sun. *Ariel's legs were so slender that both of them fit inside the iron boot, and they were squished together to make one whole new leg she couldn't walk with.* Origin: ancient Celtic Scotland.

Iron Bull: A chair with the legs of it split so the victim's legs are spread. The chair is placed on a track that it rides on, and at the end there is a pole or large spike that the victim crashes into. The chair is then taken back to the beginning, and the process is repeated until the victim is split in two. Not to be confused with **brazen bull**. *Jacob rode the one-man roller coaster that was the iron bull until he was split in two by the stripper pole on the other end.* Origin: medieval Germany.

Iron Chair: 1. See **chair of nails**. 2. An iron armchair that may not necessarily be a chair of nails. The person sits on it, and he or she is then pushed into a blazing fire. *After he sat on the chair of nails' victim's lap for some time, the executioner then pushed the chair into the roaring fireplace in front of the victim, making it into an iron chair.* 3. A collapsible iron chair the person sits in, the fire being underneath him or her. *Blaise's seven girlfriends roasted to death on iron chairs.* Origin: definitions one and two Spanish Inquisition, definition three ancient Roman.

Iron Coffin: 1. See **iron maiden**. 2. A hollow coffin with a lid slightly smaller than the sarcophagus. The victim is placed inside, and the lid slowly descends on him or her until the person is crushed to death. *The victim was crushed to death in the iron coffin over the course of several days.* Origin: medieval Italy.

Iron Collar: A metal spiked plate that fits around a person's neck. Attached to this is a cage that fits around the person's head and ends with a hook at the very top. The hook is there so a pulley can lift the person up. The metal teeth bite into the neck or jawline without slitting the throat. The pulley may bounce people in the air, swing them, or drop them suddenly. *The iron collar bit right through the girl's head and ripped her face off.* This version dates back to the Spanish Inquisition, but it was originally from ancient China. The ancient Chinese would enclose people's heads in boxes that were suspended high up so their feet couldn't touch the ground. Other variations were created for the hands, and more modern versions were made of glass instead of wood or metal. These have also made it through Asia, Europe, and other continents.

Iron Gag: A metal plate designed to fit over the lower half of a person's face. There is a tube that fits inside the mouth leading to a small hole on the outside where the person can breathe shallowly. *The inquisitioner shut up his nagging wife with the iron gag while he gave her the death sentence.* Origin: Spanish Inquisition.

Iron Maiden: A metal or wooden statue of a woman that is hollow inside but lined with spikes. It opens up, and the person is meant to walk in and be impaled to death. Sometimes there is trapdoor on the bottom of it that leads to a tunnel. Sometimes it is also lined with spikes, and it can lead to a nearby moat or river, which is used to dispose of the body. Primitive versions of this included a faceless wooden coffin with large holes on all sides and sticks that fit inside. Several people would poke the person inside with the sticks simultaneously. *The first iron maiden was modeled after inventor Nabis of Sparta's wife, Apega. Future executioners modeled it after the Virgin Mary so as to put heretics and blasphemers inside.* Origin: ancient Greece.

Iron Spider: A pair of metal claws attached to a ceiling or a fixture above the victim. They are lowered to grab people by their heads so as to poke their eyes out, or they are grabbed by their breasts, buttocks, stomach, or other fleshy areas usually after they have been heated or frozen. *The iron spider grabbed Larry by his head. Two of its claws poked his eyes out simultaneously, and it picked him up like a stuffed animal in a child's crane game.* Origin: Spanish Inquisition.

J

Jack Ketch's Kitchen: Part of the dungeon (or an actual kitchen) where severed heads are partly boiled (called parboiling) and prepared to be impaled on a stake or totem and put on display. The parboiling acts as a preservative and deters birds and other animals from eating it. *The orphan boy earned a shilling for cleaning Jack Ketch's kitchen.* Origin: medieval England.

Jack Ketch's Pippins: Hanging victims. *Jack Ketch's pippins danced the Paddington frisk for the children at Paddington Fair while he was wearing Paddington spectacles.* Origin: medieval England.

Jail: A place where criminals are kept. They are usually released after they serve their sentences or are punished. Jails do not usually have dungeons. Compare to **prison**. *Up until modern times prisons and jails were interchangeable, but nowadays the biggest difference between a jail and a prison is that a jail is more commonly used to house petty criminals, such as drunkards and prostitutes. They are usually released. A prison is for people who've committed crimes of a more serious nature, and criminals who are put in prison are usually kept for a long time and then executed.*

Jamaica Irons: See **hanging cage**.

Jerking: See **strappado**.

Jia Gun: See **kia quen**.

Jiao: Chinese for **strangulation**.

Joggs: Variant spelling of **jougs**.

Jougs: A metal collar attached to a wall by chains. The person wears the collar as a humiliation punishment and may be used in combination with other tortures. If the jougs are outside, the person could be left to die of exposure. *The deacon was put in the jougs on the outside of the church as penance.* Origin: medieval Germany.

Judas Chair: See **Judas cradle**.

Judas Cradle: A large pyramid on a tripod-like stand used for impaling people on the point. It can be used to impale (or stretch) the vagina, anus, perineum, testicles, scrotum, penis, or tailbone. Because the muscles affected naturally contract, the victim cannot relax and go to sleep, making Judas Cradle the worst form of **sleep deprivation**. Victims can support themselves by their own arms to avoid impalement, but eventually they tire and fall on the point and remain there until they can support themselves again. For a woman, when the vagina or anus is stretched, the perineum may rip and cause a **vanus**. The victims, regardless of where they are impaled from, will bleed to death from internal hemorrhaging caused by the point of the pyramid ripping through the intestines. *The Judas Cradle impaled the woman's G-spot.* Origin: ancient Roman.

Judas Seat: See **Judas cradle**.

Judas Spike: See **Judas cradle**.

Judaswiege: German for **Judas cradle**.

Judicial Birch: See **birch**.

Judicial Scold's Bridle: Another word for **branks**.

Juggs: Alternate spelling of **jougs**.

Jumping: 1. To jump on a person with an injury to prevent proper healing, usually right after the injury takes place. *After he shot him in the leg, the army man jumped on the person so he couldn't walk without a limp.* 2. To injure a person as a group of five or more people in the form of severe beatings, shootings, stabbings, sexual assault, and rape. *Mole was jumped by his friends when they found out he was betraying them.* Origin: ancient Hebrew.

K

Karavat: A beheading device consisting of a scythe-like blade attached to a long chain that circles back around. The victim puts the sharp edge of the blade on the curve of his or her neck, and the chains hang in front of the individual. The victim lies down and puts his or her feet on the chain and pushes it away. This pulls the blade and slices the neck in two. *The victim is his own executioner when the Karavat is used.* Origin: ancient India.

Keeper: Another word for **lash**.

Keel-Hauling: The act of putting a man in water and drawing him under the ship to the other side, often accompanied by a cannon firing above his head as he resurfaced. It can be considered a severe form of drowning. *The mutinous sailor died after he was keel-hauled three times.* Origin is Elizabethan England. The keel is the name of the bottom of the ship.

Kia Quen: The act of making a victim kneel over folded chairs wrapped in chains. Then three metal paddles are placed between and around the ankles, and the torturer squeezes them all together by more chains, crushing the feet and ankles. *The foot fetishist executioner enjoyed using kia quen on his victims and crippling them.* Origin: ancient China.

Kiboko: Swahili dialect for hippopotamus, which is their name for the **sjambok** because it is most commonly made from hippopotamus hides.

Kick: To strike a person with the foot or leg, similar to **punch**. *David kicked Destiny's severed head like a soccer ball.* Origin: ancient Mesopotamian.

Kiss the Gunner's Daughter: To be bent over a cannon's muzzle and flogged. Lighting the cannon so as to disembowel the person after the flogging was optional. *The buccaneer kissed the gunner's daughter, and then the cannon was lit to blow his intestines out over the oggin.* Origin: medieval England.

Kneecapping: To remove or maim the kneecaps so they no longer function. *If Oswald had only paid his bookie he would not have gotten kneecapped.* Origin: ancient Roman.

Knee Splitter: A collapsible square frame lined with nails in which kneecaps, elbows, shoulders, hips, or other large joints can be placed in and crushed, crippling the person. *Garrett couldn't walk anymore because he was kneecapped by the knee splitter.* Origin: Spanish Inquisition.

Knife: A short blade attached to a handle. The blade may be either curved or straight and may be of any size, but all knives are made to be held by the handle by using one hand. Compare to **sword**. *Knives can be used in most tortures, but most especially the thousand cuts, beyond a thousand cuts, twenty-four cuts, and similar techniques.* Origin: ancient Mesopotamian.

Knoet: Dutch for **knout**.

Knoot: Variant spelling of **knout**.

Knotted Rope: A piece of rope with a knot in it that goes over an eyeball and is then tightened, putting pressure on the eye and causing eventual blindness. This is a form of **abacination**. Another variant of it is to simply blindfold the person with a rope around both eyes and tighten it. *The knotted rope pushed Charles's eyeball through the eye socket and next to his brain.* This form of abacination dates back to medieval England.

Knout: Literally means **whip** in Russian. It is a type of whip consisting of multiple rawhide lashes attached to a long handle. There are hooks at the ends of the tails, and these sometimes have metal wires intertwined in the lashes. There are different variations of this. One has a lash of rawhide sixteen inches long attached to a wooden handle more than eight inches long. The lash ends in a metal ring that is attached to another leather lash ending in a hook. Another variation is basically the **cat o' nine tails**, but it has wire. *Ivan died after twenty-five lashes of the knout.* Origin: ancient Mongolian.

Knuckledusters: See **brass knuckles**.

Knuckle Knives: See **brass knuckles**.

Knut: Variant spelling of **knout**.

Knute: German for **knout**.

Knut Piska: A **whip** made from knotted ropes. *The Knut Piska was adopted by the Tartar people and later brought into Russia as the knout.* Origin: ancient Sweden.

Knutr: Old Norse for **knout**.

Kurbash: Arabic for **whip**. In Egypt and North Africa, it most commonly refers to the **sjambok**. The Arabic language does not appear to differentiate different types of whips.

L

Ladder Rack: A variant of the standard **rack** that is vertical and resembles a ladder. *Strapped to the rungs of the ladder rack, Theresa's shoulders dislocated as the cranks turned mercilessly.* Origin: medieval Austria.

Lash: The end of a **whip** that strikes the target. *The lash is the part that either makes a whip great or unreliable.* Origin: ancient Egyptian.

Lasso: Another name for a **noose**.

Lastersteine: German for **whirligig**.

Lead Coffin: A coffin made of lead in which a person was thrown into a body of water to drown. An alternate version was to simply wrap the person in lead sheets and then throw him or her into the water to drown. *The four stonemasons were put in lead coffins and drowned because they refused to do their jobs.* Origin: ancient Roman.

Lead Sprinkler: A holy water sprinkler filled with red-hot iron filings used to burn people on random body parts, particularly heretics. *The lead sprinkler may have also been a precursor to the modern salt and pepper shakers.* Origin: Spanish Inquisition.

Leg Screw: See **iron boot**.

Lethal Injection: The administration of poison into the body with a syringe. *The angel of death administered the lethal injection to the dying patient.* Origin is the modern United States. The lethal injection is a descendant of forcing a person to drink poison as an execution practiced since ancient Greek times. This is also a pharmacological torture if the person either survives or suffers before death.

Light Control: 1. To shut off the lights unexpectedly to frighten the prisoners. 2. To unexpectedly turn on the bright lights after being in the dark to frighten and temporarily blind and disorient the prisoners. 3. To turn the lights on and off repeatedly in a flickering effect in the hopes of frightening and/or temporarily blinding the prisoners, perhaps during physical tortures. *Being afraid of the dark, Amber screamed the loudest whenever the warden exercised light control and plummeted the whole prison into a suffocating darkness.* Origin: modern Austria.

Ling-Chy: Chinese for **thousand cuts** or **slicing process**.

Little Ease: A box in which a person's body is folded to fit inside. Then the person is either left there to die of starvation, or the box is filled with scorpions, bees, snakes, or other insects. The person is then bitten or stung to death while a group of interrogators makes loud noises to frighten all the creatures inside the box. Alternatively little ease also describes closet-like cells that have no room for the person to change positions (e.g., from standing to sitting or lying down, from sitting or squatting to standing or laying down, or from laying down to sitting up or standing). *The pirate was stung to death by scorpions in the little ease box.* Origin: medieval England.

Little White Dragon: A white plastic pipe used for **flagellation.** *The little white dragon is a simple plastic pipe, but it can do a lot of damage.* Origin: modern China.

Litupa: Another word for **sjambok**.

Liu: Chinese for **exile** and "forbidden to return to one's birthplace."

Longe Whip: A **stock whip** with a very long lash. The shaft is four to five inches long, and the lash is just as long or longer. *Other than the very long lash, longe whips generally look like most other types of whips.* Origin: medieval France.

Lowe: Nickname given to an executioner's assistant. He is called so because it literally means *lion*, and the executioner's assistant would roar loudly while he brought the accused before the judge. *The Lowe roared like a lion as he dragged the frightened prisoner to certain doom.* Origin: medieval Germany.

Lud's Bulwark: Nickname for Ludgate Prison. *The prisoner cursed Lud for the creation of the bulwark he was stuck in.* Origin: medieval England.

Lunette: The part of the guillotine that restrains the person's head. *Louis laid his neck in the lunette and waited to die.* Origin: French Revolution.

M

Malay Boot: See **iron boot**.

Manacle: A pair of rings, metal band, chain, **handcuffs,** or **shackles** used to secure a person's ankles or wrists. *He was soundly detained in manacles.* Origin: ancient Hebrew.

Mancuerda: The act of wrapping a person's arms with barbed wire or a tight cord six to eight times and squeezing tightly. *The muscleman's arms were bound in Mancuerda cords, which were hooked to a car that then drove off, dragging the man to death.* Origin is ancient Roman. This originates from an early form of the torture rack in which the victim's whole body was covered in cords that continuously tightened. It also restrained the victim to the table.

Man Humbler: Two arch-shaped pieces of wood that are attached to each other and open like a book. The base of a man's scrotum is sandwiched between the curves, and the sides are secured behind the thighs and at the base of his buttocks. The wearer must keep his legs folded forward. Any effort to straighten the legs (even slightly) will pull directly on the scrotum and cause extreme discomfort. The device is designed to restrict a prisoner's movements. *The man humbler is basically like handcuffs for the scrotum.* Origin: ancient Greece.

Mannaia: A precursor to the guillotine in which the victim had to kneel to be beheaded by the scythe-like blade. *The mannaia was* *inspired by the diele, and it was later an inspiration for the guillotine.* Origin: medieval Italian.

Manx Hazel Birch: See **birch**.

Marketplace: A place that is not only a store or a bazaar but a very public place to punish or execute criminals. It was the most popular place for the scaffold in the Middle Ages along with **town square**. *Not only can one go shopping in a marketplace, but one can also enjoy the entertainment that comes with watching criminals get what's coming.* Origin: ancient Hebrew.

Maroon: To **exile** a person. *Maroon has two other definitions. It is a dark shade of red with a tint of brown, and it is also an insult to a person, meaning stupid as in the saying "What a maroon." One can also say, "The maroon in the maroon-colored shirt was marooned on the deserted island."* The word *maroon*, regardless of definition, originates in medieval England. The practice of marooning or exiling people originates in ancient Mesopotamia.

Mask of Infamy: Another term for **mask of shame** because infamous people were made to wear it.

Mask of Shame: A metal mask designed to cover the person's head like a pair of **branks.** Metal balls meant to fit into the person's mouth and one nostril are attached inside to keep the victim silent. The mask is designed to resemble an animal that suits the person's crime. A pig would mean gluttony or a man who has acted like one or treated his wife badly. A cow would signal laziness, donkey foolishness, and rabbit for eavesdropping. Other masks of shame include masks that look like vultures or crows, dragons, bearded men, women with big ears and long tongues to symbolize gossiping and noisiness, and women or men with long noses to symbolize nosiness or being stuck up. There were many designs for masks of shame. They could look like anything the person making them wanted, and the masks could look very artistic. The same could be said for many torture devices, including the **branks**, **pear of anguish**, and generally most shaming devices. *Everyone laughed at Greta as she was escorted around town, wearing a mask of shame.* Origin: medieval Germany.

Mate of Death: A nickname for an executioner. *The mate of death executed many criminals.* Origin: medieval German.

Matwasat: African for type-three **female circumcision** in which all external female genitalia are removed. A stick or rock salt is put inside the vaginal opening, and the victim's legs are tied from hips to ankles for fifty to forty days. During this period of time the wounds heal themselves across the vulva to form a wall of flesh and scab. The stick or salt creates the hole for urination and painful sexual intercourse. *Matwasat was used to make sexual intercourse unpleasant so the victim wouldn't commit adultery after marriage.* Origin: ancient Africa.

Mazzatello: A large mallet used to smash the head of the victim. *Giordano's head exploded into tiny pieces as his head was pulverized by the Mazzatello.* Origin: medieval Italian.

Menstrualphagia: The forcing or coercing someone to drink menstrual blood. Compare to **coprophagia** and **urophagia**. *The misandrous lesbian's favorite method of emasculating men was to paint their thighs with her menstrual blood and then force them into mentrualphagia by drinking straight from the source.* Origin: ancient Mesopotamian.

Mill: The same contraption that has been used to grind grain into flour for centuries was also used to grind people as a form of **crushing**. *Emperor Maximian had St. Victor ground to death in a mill after he was savagely tortured by an angry mob.* The ancient Mesopotamians were inventors of the first mill, but the ancient Romans were the first documented people who were using it to grind people.

Mill Wheel: A water-mill wheel with a victim tied to the paddles and spinning. *Every time Arnold's head surfaced from the water, the soldier stuck his bayonet in him, and then the mill wheel cycled again.* Origin: medieval Hungary.

Mo: Chinese for forehead **tattoo** as a way of marking a person for a crime just like **branding.** The forehead tattoo was made from indelible ink.

Mock Execution: To make people believe that they are being executed but then not follow through with it. For example, a torturer could hold a gun to their heads in a **firing squad** style and then pull the trigger several times only to reveal the gun is empty. Then the torturer can send them back to their cells. The torturer could also put them in an electric chair and not flip the switch. He could give them shots of morphine or other medications and tell them that it's the lethal injection. *Michael committed suicide in prison after he suffered a mock execution.* Origin: ancient Mesopotamian.

Monkey Sucking a Peach Dry: To coerce a monkey into giving a victim a blow job. The monkey eats the person's genitalia, thighs, and buttocks. This is a form of **castration**. *The zoophile's dream turned into a nightmare as a pissed-off monkey sucked his peach dry.* Origin: ancient Chinese.

Moses' Law: To flog or strike someone exactly thirty-nine times with any flogging device. *In the Old Testament's book of Leviticus, it is prescribed to never beat someone more than forty times, but historically people who were beaten and flogged suffered much more.* Origin: ancient Hebrew.

Mouth Opener: A device with hooks on cords that are inserted in a person's mouth to keep the mouth open as a prelude to the **tongue tearer, tongue stretcher, tooth extraction**, and things a dentist might do to someone. Modern mouth openers' hooks are made of plastic or rubber and are mainly used on people who are afraid of dental procedures or have difficulty keeping their mouths open for an extended period of time, such as children. Another form of mouth opener is a metal hoop that is inserted into the mouth and can expand with a crank. It may expand so far as to break the person's jaw. *The evil dentist exercised all forms of oral torture accompanied with the mouth opener.* Origin: Spanish Inquisition.

Mouth Pear: See **pear of anguish**.

Mnigolo: Malinke dialect for hippopotamus, which is their name for the **sjambok** because it is most commonly made from hippopotamus hides.

Murga: Means *rooster* in both Hindi and Urdu. There are seven types of Murga—squatting, standing, swaying, sitting, heels touching, riding, and parade. Squatting is when the person squats with knees together, buttocks raised in the air, arms hooked around the knees, and ears squeezed. Standing Murga is when the person's legs are straight, but the buttocks are expected to be raised in the air as high as possible. Swaying Murga is when the person alternates from standing Murga to sitting at intervals. Sitting Murga is when the person sits on the floor with legs stretched out in front and forearms are rested firmly on the ground in front between the legs. Heels touching Murga is the same as either sitting or standing except the heels have to be touching at all times. Riding Murga is the same as Murga parade except the person is expected to carry another person on his or her back. Murga parade is the same as standing Murga except the person is expected to walk, sometimes outside under the sun. People will be beaten if they cannot maintain the positions they are expected to maintain. *It is called Murga because the person's body posture makes him or her look like a rooster with tail feathers in the air.* Origin: ancient India.

Murgha: Alternate spelling for **murga**.

Mute's Bridle: See **iron gag**.

Mutilation: The act of disfiguring people, altering their appearances through injuries or damage to the body. *Brandon was badly mutilated.* Origin: ancient Mesopotamian.

Mutilation Shears: A pair of shears used to cut off small body parts, such as fingers and toes. *Mutilation shears were popular for cutting off fingers and toes after they were crushed by a hand crusher and a toe breaker.* Origin: Spanish Inquisition.

Myrnyx: Japanese for "limb pearer." This was another form of the **tekko**. *There wasn't much difference between the Myrnyx and the tekko.* Origin: feudal Japan.

N

Nail: A small spike with a flat head. *Handy Hans pounded the nails into the victim's body like she was a piece of wood.* Origin: ancient Mesopotamia.

Nail Insertion: To insert red-hot filings or nails under fingernails, sometimes as a prelude to **denailing** or as a part of that process. However, oftentimes nail insertion is used as a torture by itself. *The circus freak used nail insertion on herself and then scratched a chalkboard.* Also compare to **tablilla**. Origin: Spanish Inquisition.

Nail through the Ear: 1. To pound a long iron nail through the ear and into the brain. *Bacha crucified Ali Ahmed to the ground and drove a nail through the ear and into his brain.* 2. To pound a nail through a person's earlobe into something wooden such as stockades, a table, wall, or door and then to rip it out. *Jacob had a bloody scar on his earlobe as a reminder of what he'd done to deserve public humiliation in the stocks plus a nail through the ear.* Origin: first definition modern Afghanistan, second definition Ancient Hebrew.

Naked Pyramid: A pile of naked (and usually all-male) prisoners stacked on top of one another, all of them penetrating one another's anuses, except for whoever is on top, roughly in the shape of a pyramid. This is considered a form of mass **sexual assault**. *The prison guards subdued all the prisoners and threw them on top of one another in a naked pyramid.* Americans invented this in modern Afghanistan.

National Razor: The guillotine. It was called this by the French during the Revolution.

Neck Grabber: A large pair of pincers with the grabbing part lined with spikes. It wraps around the victim's neck and may then be used to either drag the person into prison or strangle him or her to death. It can also be a collar lined with spikes with a pole attached to it that is used to drag people or force them into humiliating positions. *The neck grabber was also used to control slaves in colonial America and other places.* Origin: Spanish Inquisition.

Necklacing: To place a car tire around a person's neck and light it on fire, causing the person to either suffocate or burn if he or she didn't suffocate fast enough. *Aristide endorsed the necklacing of secret police in an interview over the radio.* Origin: modern South Africa.

Neck Violin: A guitar with a hole all the way through the body and two holes in the neck. A person wears it with the neck in the largest hole and the wrists in the two smaller ones. *The handle of the neck violin was used to drag the man out in public while a cudgel was used to bash his head at the same time.* Origin: Spanish Inquisition.

Neckweed: British nickname for the **noose.**

Night Watch: nickname for **Judas cradle.**

Noise-Maker's Fife: A collar with a long handle that looks like a flute. The body of this handle is divided into three bars that can be tightened. The victim's neck is put in the collar, and the fingers are placed between the bars on either side. It ultimately looks like the person is playing a large flute. *The bad karaoke singer was laughed at more when she was forced to wear the noise-maker's fife for being a bad musician.* Origin: Spanish Inquisition.

Noose: A piece of rope used to hang or strangle someone. *The serial killer's favorite weapon was the noose.* Origin: ancient Hebrew.

Nose Slit: To cut the cartilage between the nostrils so the two nostrils become one large one. *Ali Babar got his nose slit because he was caught raping a camel.* Origin: ancient Byzantine Empire.

Nubbing: Hanging. *The thief was nubbing.* Origin: medieval England.

O

Oil of the Birch: Irish for **birch**.

Oil of the Hazel: Irish for a **hazel rod**.

Old Smoky: Another word for the **electric chair**.

Oopherectomy: The scientific word for **castration**.

Oral Pear: See **pear of anguish**.

Orba: Comes from Old Italian, meaning blinded. An orba is a tiny, one-man cell with no light, windows, holes, not even a bed or a toilet. The prisoner must urinate and defecate on the floor or walls, which are never cleaned. *Marco was shut up in an orba while he was awaiting trial.* Origin: medieval Italian.

Ostracizing: To ignore a person as a group of peers, community, or society as punishment for a social crime. *Carrie was ostracized by her friends for getting them into trouble.* Origin: ancient Greece.

Ostrakios: Literally means oyster shells in ancient Greek but was used to reference brick tiles on houses. These were sometimes alternatively used to hack off limbs as a method of execution. *Emperor Cyril ordered the martyrdom of the Gnostic Saint Hypatia of Alexandria by having soldiers smash her shoulder and hip joints with Ostenkios bricks* *until her arms and legs were eventually hacked off in a brutal manner.* Origin: ancient Greece.

Oubliette: French word for **orba.**

Outcast: A person who is ignored by a group of peers, community, or society as punishment for a social crime; a person who is **ostracized.** *Carrie became an outcast because she couldn't fit into normal social standards.* The word *outcast* originates in Victorian England from the word *outcaste,* meaning one who has been rejected by one's own caste system in India for a crime or meaning a person who does not belong to a caste in India. The act of ostracizing criminals as a punishment originates in ancient Greece.

Outlaw: 1. Another word for **criminal.** 2. To make something illegal by banning the action, process, or item. *The outlaws made their way to the next county with the stolen bank money. Alcohol was outlawed during prohibition.* The word outlaw in both senses of the word originates in Old Norse dialect, meaning *banished.* Outlaws or outlawing things have been around since the dawn of humanity in ancient Mesopotamia.

Overseer: 1. A person who masters slaves or prisoners. *The overseer was sadistic.* 2. A person in a pillory, overlooking the crowds. *The overseer couldn't bear seeing the crowds.* Origin: medieval England.

Over the Cannon's Muzzle: To load a cannon, tie a person's body across it, and then fire the cannon, disemboweling the victim or possibly splitting him or her in half. *The captain ordered the mutineer to be blown over the cannon's muzzle.* Origin: medieval England.

Oxygen Deprivation: To suffocate or asphyxiate a person for brief moments of time or to execute the person by means of depriving oxygen. *The simpleton suffered more brain damage from oxygen deprivation.* Origin: ancient Mesopotamian.

P

Paddington Fair: Medieval nickname for Tyburn, London, especially on a hanging day, because it teemed with hundreds of people like a carnival or circus. Tyburn was a place in central London where most public executions took place. Public executions tended to draw massive crowds who enjoyed watching people suffer and die. *The children enjoyed seeing grown men die at Paddington Fair.* Origin: medieval England.

Paddington Frisk: The spasms hanging victims give when choking. This looks like a dance. *Jack Ketch's pippins danced the Paddington frisk for the children at Paddington Fair while he was wearing Paddington spectacles.* Origin: medieval England.

Paddington Spectacles: Blindfold. *Jack Ketch's pippins danced the Paddington frisk for the children at Paddington Fair while he was wearing Paddington spectacles.* Origin: medieval England.

Paia: Turkish for pointed stake, which was used for **impaling**.

Palace of Illusion: A large room where one or more victims are placed. It is like the **sweatbox** in that it is deliberately overheated. There are also iron treelike props and sounds that make people believe they are in an African jungle. The lights can be put out to simulate nighttime. The victims hear animal noises and think they are going to be attacked, but there are no animals. The victim also hears a babbling brook or a waterfall but can only find a realistic painting of one at the far side of the room. Right next to this is another tree with two nooses hanging from it, one of them being vacant, a corpse using the other one. When victims have had enough psychological torture, are not willing to duel any other victims, and don't want to die of hunger, thirst, or heat exhaustion, they can use the noose to kill themselves since they probably won't make it out. A palace of illusion could also be made to simulate another environment depending on who designs it. *Raul and his friend went insane and believed they were in a jungle because they had spent too much time in the palace of illusion.* Origin: ancient India.

Palioly's Pear: See **pear of anguish**. It was sometimes called this because it was probably named for the inventor.

Palestinian Hanging: Politically incorrect nickname for **strappado**.

Palestinian Crucifixion: Another politically incorrect nickname for **strappado** because it is believed to be a sanctioned punishment in Palestine. When a person dies of strappado, it is the same cause of death that kills someone who is crucified in that the person suffocates.

Palierdo: Means *polygon* in Spanish. It refers to any shape that can be classified as a polygon, including a pyramid. Palierdo is the Spanish name for **Judas cradle**. *Palierdo is the Spanish translation of the Italian Palledro.* Origin: Spanish Inquisition.

Palledro: To rupture veins and tissue without drawing blood, using a form of **Judas cradle** or something similar. *The Inquisitors inflicted the Palledro on Campanella in hopes of getting him to renounce his heresy.* Origin: medieval Italy.

Parboiling: To partially boil something or not completely boil something while one is cooking it in hot oil or water, cumin seed, and salt. *The severed heads were parboiled in Jack Ketch's kitchen prior to being put on display.* Origin: medieval England.

Parrilla: Spanish for **electrocution**.

Parrot's Perch: Two metal bars a certain distance from each other. A person's knees rest on the lower bar, and the armpits rest on the upper bar with his or her hands behind the back. This usually takes place in a large cage, and the victim looks like a parrot on its perch. *Juan had his body painted, and he wore a costume. Consequently he did look like a parrot as he rode on the parrot's perch.* Origin: modern Brazil.

Partial Pudenda: A type of **chastity belt** that only covers the vagina and is also called the Florentine girdle. *Hephaestus made Aphrodite wear a partial pudenda so she would stop having an affair with Ares.* Origin: ancient Greece.

Pasiphae and the Bull: A recreation of an ancient Greek myth in which the queen of Crete gave birth to the Minotaur by attaching a naked woman's vagina to a live bull's head. The result is that she is gored to death by the horns and possibly split in two. *They had to get a new actress every time they wanted to perform Pasiphae and the Bull.* Origin: ancient Roman.

Patterned Birch: See **birch**.

Patterned Cane: See **birch**.

Patriotic Shortener: See **guillotine**.

Pau de Arara: Portuguese for **parrot's perch**, literally translated as "perch of parrot."

Pear: See **pear of anguish**.

Pear of Anguish: A metal pear with the ability to expand by twisting the stem. This is inserted into orifices such as the mouth, vagina, and anus, and the expansion causes the orifice to expand and rip until pulverized.

If used in the mouth, the pear will knock out and break all teeth and severely dislocate the jaw and palette. *Jack shouldn't have tried to eat the pear of anguish. Now he can't talk or eat.* Origin: Spanish Inquisition.

Pear of Confession: See **pear of anguish**.

Pegging: The act of sodomizing or raping a person by using a strap-on dildo, usually done by a woman. *Grizelda pegged Kylie in order to rape her.* Origin: ancient Greece.

Peine Forte et Dure: To put a board on top of a naked victim on the ground and then to put stones on top of this until the victim is crushed to death. *Giles was sentenced to peine forte et dure for refusing to plead guilty in court.* The phrase *peine forte et dure* is French for "press to death," but human presses have been around since ancient Rome.

Penal Servitude: See **bondage**.

Penalty: Another word for **punishment**.

Pendola: Spanish for **pendulum**.

Pendulum: 1. An ax attached to a chain that swings down from a pulley to an awaiting victim. It is called a pendulum because the ax swings like a pendulum in an old-fashioned grandfather clock. *Edgar Allan Poe famously wrote about the pendulum in "The Pit and the Pendulum."* 2. Another word for **strappado** because the victim swings like the pendulum. *The swinging pendulum victim accidentally kicked his torturer in the head.* Origin: Spanish Inquisition for both definitions.

Peng: Chinese for boiling alive.

Penis Chastity Cage: A **chastity belt** designed for men to wear. It consists of several metal rings all connected. These make a sheath that goes over the limp penis. This sheath is attached to a belt that fits snuggly around the waist. The ring sheath is designed to prevent the penis from becoming erect as the person is being aroused. Others can try to instigate an erection on purpose, as that would cause significant discomfort or pain. Just like its female counterpart, the person can urinate through the penis chastity cage. *The penis chastity cage is the male equivalent of the chastity belt for women.* Origin: ancient Greece.

Penology: The study of crime, punishment, and all things associated with them. *If it weren't for penology, this book would never have been written.* Origin: ancient Roman.

People's Avenger: See **guillotine**.

Pere Lebrun: The French term for **necklacing** someone.

Peroneal Strike: To hit a person above the knee on the side with a baton or like object. In that place there is a nerve that helps coordinate a person's legs when he or she is walking or running. Hitting a person there correctly will knock the victim down. Hitting the person there repeatedly will cause permanent disability. *Ali died from receiving hundreds of peroneal strikes in a row for several hours.* Origin: ancient Mesopotamian.

Petalism: A fancy word for **exile**.

Pharmacological Torture: 1. The act of drugging a prisoner and allowing the side effects to take the form of torture. *The ancient Chinese used pharmacological torture to give a woman drugs that bestowed instant old age.* 2. The denial of drugs to an addict and allowing the withdrawal symptoms to be torture. *The modern prison guards used pharmacological torture to deny the painkiller addict his favorite pills.* 3. The administration of parasites to a person so that he or she becomes severely sick or dies. *The fat girl force-fed tapeworm eggs to the skinny girl as a pharmacological torture.* Origin: ancient Chinese.

Phobia Exploitation: The act of using something a person is afraid of against him or her. For example, a person with arachnophobia can be left in a room filled with spiders or a **cave of roses**. A person with claustrophobia can be crushed up or shut up in an **iron maiden**. A person afraid of drowning can be put in a room that slowly floods or dunked by a **ducking stool**, etc. *Since most people are afraid of death and suffering, a great way to exploit phobia in anyone is a mock execution.* Origin: ancient Mesopotamian.

Physical Punishment: See **corporal punishment.**

Physical Violence: See **beating.**

Picana: Spanish for **cattle prod.**

Picnic Basket: Wicker receptacle for the severed head at the guillotine. *The head fell in the picnic basket.* Origin: French Revolution.

Picquet: To hang someone by one thumb and have one foot resting on a sharp stake. The person has to choose between having their thumb dislocated or their foot skewered. Oftentimes both take place. *The best way to endure the picquet is to rest the tough, callous part of the heel on the stake.* Origin: medieval England.

Piercing: To skewer a small body part. In colonial America and medieval England, this was done on the tongue for the purposes of marking that person for a minor crime. Also people had their ears pierced by having their ears nailed to **stocks**, wooden doors, and walls. It serves the same purpose as **branding** and **tattooing**. *In colonial America, piercing was a punishment. Nowadays it is an alternative form of fashion and practiced on most small body parts.* Origin: medieval England.

Pillory: Another word for **stockades.**

Pincher: A large device similar to pliers that traps small pieces of flesh in its claws and squeezes tightly. *In medieval France, having red-hot pinchers applied to the arms and genitalia was a precursor to quartering by horses.* Origin: ancient Roman.

Piquet: Alternate spelling of **picquet**. This is not to be confused with the card game or the archaic military term for watchmen, both of which are spelled the same way.

Pitchcapping: To pour hot pitch or tar on a person's head, put a metal cone on it, allow the tar to cool, and then rip it all off, scalping the person. *A victim of pitchcapping is called a croppy. This is also a type of hairstyle in which the person is bald on top, and the word is slang for a rebel in Ireland as well.* The British invented this in Celtic Ireland, and they used it against Irish people a millennium ago.

Pitchfork: A two or three-pronged impaling implement. The prongs emerge out of one shaft and may be used to stab people. *Every citizen in the angry mob carried a torch and a pitchfork.* Origin is ancient Mesopotamian. The pitchfork's original purpose was a farming tool used to toss hay.

Plank: 1. See **slapstick**. 2. To make people walk on a plank attached to a ship or boat and to push them off or coerce them to jump off so they drown in the ocean. *Pirates famously executed one another by making them walk the plank. They most likely drown, or they are exiled.* Origin: ancient China.

Pleti: A type of whip similar to a **knout whip** with multiple lashes that each split into three. Each of those tails ends in lead balls. *Czar Nicholas I abolished the knout in 1845 and replaced it with the Pleti.* Origin: medieval Russia.

Pliniewinkies: Scottish word for **thumbscrews**.

Pocket Snake Whip: A miniature **snake whip** that is supposed to be small enough to fit in a pocket. It is four to six feet long. *Chad liked to take his pocket snake whip with him wherever he went. He didn't feel safe without it.* Origin: medieval England.

Poison: To give a cup of poison to a condemned criminal in hopes that he will drink it. This was the precursor to the modern **lethal injection**. *Aristotle was poisoned by hemlock, and the executioner didn't want to give it to him.* Origin: ancient Greece.

Poker: A large skewer, spit, or a common fireplace poker that may be heated or frozen and used to impale or skewer a limb, genitalia, or other nonlethal nerve endings. It can also be used to internally burn someone by putting it down someone's throat or up the person's anus or vagina. Alternatively it can be put in the eyes as **abacination**. It may also be put deep inside the ears to break the eardrum and cause **deafness**. *When one uses a red-hot poker to abacinate someone, one must be careful not to put it too far, or you will impale the brain and kill the person.* Origin: ancient Philistine.

Polish Bike Ride: A bicycle without the seat. The person is forced to be seated on top of it with the metal impaling the victim's anus. It is vaguely similar in concept to the **Judas cradle**. *Kaz tried to ride away from his captors on the Polish bike ride, but he died when he was impaled.* Origin: modern Poland.

Pope's Pear: See **pear of anguish**. It was sometimes called this because Pope Innocent XIII endorsed the use of this device anally against homosexuals during the Spanish Inquisition.

Popper: Another word for **lash**. It is called this because of the popping noises it sometimes makes.

Pranger: A collar with shackles attached to it on a short chain. The person wears the collar on the neck and the shackles on the ankles. The short chain causes the person to squat low, and the person's hands are tied behind his or her back with handcuffs. *Tiffany fell flat on her face as she waddled because she was wearing the pranger.* Origin: medieval Germany.

Prank: A practical joke or mischievous act designed to make one or more people doubt their sanity or possibly cause them to go insane. *Pranks may or may not be harmless depending on how deeply it affects the person and whether or not the person is physically harmed from it.* Origin: ancient Mesopotamian.

Prankster: A psychologically sadistic person who plays pranks or practical jokes on other people, plays mind games on them, or traps them in ways that affect them psychologically. *In Native American mythology, the Coyote is both a prankster and a hero who acts according to his own agenda and unconventional moral codes.* Origin: ancient Mesopotamian.

Premature Burial: See **buried alive**.

Pressure Points: Places on the human body that are more sensitive to pressure and injury than others. Skilled torturers and executioners often exploit such as joints and the groin area. *The massage therapist turned torturer exploited his patient's pressure points in a most agonizing way.* Origin: ancient Chinese.

Prison: A place where criminals are kept, interrogated, tortured, and sometimes executed for crimes. Compare to **dungeon** and **jail**. *The miscreant was in prison for murder.* Origin: ancient Mesopotamian.

Prison Forte et Dure: French for **starvation** in prison. Sometimes the victims weren't completely starved but were severely malnourished so that they eventually died.

Prison of Darkness: Solitary confinement in a black hole. This could be accompanied by **evil noise** or drastic temperature changes. *Bingam* *was kept in the prison of darkness for weeks, blasted by loud noises and extremely cold temperatures.* Origin: modern Iraq.

Psychological Torture: To torture a person mentally or verbally without using physical violence. For example, one could threaten physical violence, **blackmailing**, name-calling, etc. The most extreme forms of psychological tortures are **palace of illusion, mock execution,** and **phobia exploitation**. *She had no physical power over them, so she got her answers and her revenge through psychological tortures.* Origin: ancient Mesopotamian.

Public Humiliation: To shame or put someone down in public, to mock or laugh at a person, to pick on a person as a group. Devices have been created to shame people in public for minor crimes they have committed or vices, such as **stockades, barrel pillory, floggings, exposure, hanging cage, noise-maker's fife, neck grabber, bell collar, mask of shame,** etc. Public humiliation often means people get to throw things like rotten food and fecal matter at the person. *The drug addict killed himself after enduring weeks of public humiliation in the stockades.* Origin: ancient Mesopotamian.

Punch: To hit someone with a closed fist, similar to **kick**. *He punched her face until she was disfigured.* Origin: ancient Hebrew.

Punisher: A person who executes the infliction of a penalty for a crime committed. Basically this person is a **torturer**. *An executioner could be considered a punisher if he used both corporal and capital punishments to bring criminals to justice.* Origin: ancient Mesopotamian.

Punishment: The infliction of a penalty for a crime committed. Compare to **discipline**. *His punishment was more than he could bear.* Origin: ancient Mesopotamian.

Punjab Lasso: See **noose** or **hanging**.

Pulley: A wheel with a cord around it. One end of the cord is controlled by a lever, and the other has a person hanging from it. A pulley is used for **strappado**. A pulley can also hang people by their wrists so their arms are above their heads, or they can be upside down and strung up from their ankles for long periods of time so their blood rushes to their heads. *Countess Bathory used a pulley to string up young girls upside down by their ankles, and then she would gut them, collect their blood in a bathtub, and bathe naked in it.* Origin: ancient Roman.

Purple Robe: After people were severely flogged, their nakedness was covered up by a purple robe for a couple hours. The robe was a shaming device, and after that, the robe was ripped off the person. Their wounds congealed to the fabric while they wore it, so when it was ripped off, exposing them again, it also ripped their scabs so that they bled again. *Christ was forced to wear a purple robe after his flogging. He also wore it while he was wearing the crown of thorns because he was "king of the Jews" and these things were Pilate's ways of mocking him. He was crucified shortly afterward.* Origin: ancient Hebrew.

Q

Qapani: Arabic for **sleep deprivation**.

Qilinbian: Literally means "unicorn whip" in Chinese. It was a metal whip with a fifteen-centimeter handle made from a steel chain wrapped in leather. The lash consisted of steel rods decreasing in size and linked by smaller rings. The lash is 150 to 180 centimeters and attached to a fall and cracker that are each one to two kilograms. *The Qilinbian is one of the few Chinese inventions not created in ancient times.* Origin: modern China.

Qishi: Chinese for marketplace, which they used as a **scaffold**.

Quartering: To cut a person into four pieces with dismemberment or to cut off the limbs with a sword, saw, ax, scythe, or another tool used to cut. *Quartering is a third of hanging, drawing, and quartering.* Origin: ancient Roman.

Quartering by boats: To tie a person's arms to the stern of one boat and legs to the stern of another and then to have the boats row in opposite directions, dismembering the person after the tendons in all limbs have been cut. *Spanish pirates were quartered by boats because the punishment fit the crime, but it did not happen very often.* Origin: medieval Spain.

Quartering by Camels: To tie a person's left arm to one camel with a rope or chain, the right arm to another, the left leg to another, and the right leg to another or to have both arms tied to one camel and both legs to another camel. Then all the different camels are driven in opposite directions until the person is dismembered, usually after the tendons in all limbs have been cut. *The prophet was quartered by camels for angering the Sultan.* Origin: ancient Saudi Arabia.

Quartering by Horses: To tie a person's left arm to one horse with a rope or chain, the right arm or another, the left leg to another, and the right leg to another or to have both arms tied to one horse and both legs to another horse. Then all the different horses be driven in opposite directions until the person is dismembered, usually after the tendons in all limbs have been cut. *Francis was quartered by horses for assassinating the king.* Origin: medieval France.

Quartering by Two Trees: See **tree tearer**.

Question: To question someone is to **interrogate** the person. Questioning a person for several hours with no breaks is a form of **sleep deprivation**. When several questioners take turns doing so, that is called a **conveyor**. The Spanish Inquisition was also sometimes called "The Question." *The inquisitors put Esmeralda to the question for hours about a crime she did not commit and knew nothing about.* Origin: Spanish Inquisition.

Questioner: A **torturer** or **inquisitor**, one who questions people suspected of crimes or witnesses to them. *Nowadays in the modern United States, Europe, and Australia, the policemen who are questioners are not allowed to enhance their interrogations with physical torture.* This terminology originates with the Spanish Inquisition, but the idea of questioning people concerning crimes originates with ancient Mesopotamia.

Quills: Long spikes that porcupines grow naturally. They can be harvested by people and use to **stab** felons as a punishment. *In the*

Middle Ages, quills were also used to create fountain pens for writing. Origin: medieval France.

Quirt: A **stock whip** with two lashes usually made of leather, buffalo, or cowhide. The center of these lashes is a leather bag filled with lead. The handle is made from braided rawhide leather or kangaroo hide. It is stiff but flexible. *The biggest difference between the quirt and other types of stock whips are the double lashes.* Origin: medieval England.

R

Rack: A table, bench, or ladder on which a person is tied and is pulled by all limbs until they are dismembered. Some racks have nails in them and are like the **bed of nails**, but the victims are stretched. Some have a miniature **revolving drum** in the center that strips away flesh as the victim is stretched. Some racks are like the **gridiron**, in which the body of it is made of iron bars and a fire cooks the victim underneath as the person is stretched on top of it. The rack is often used in combination with other tortures, such as **flogging,** torching the victims' armpits, sides, feet, and genitalia, ripping out their rib cages with hooks, **denailing, sexual assault, thousand cuts, beyond a thousand cuts, cat's paws, iron spider,** and whatever else the torturers can think of to make people as miserable as possible. *Julietta was stretched on the rack and martyred.* Origin: ancient Greece.

Ragging: See **hazing**.

Raman Whip: A type of **stock whip** used in Canada, related to the **rose whip**. *The Raman whip is one of the more generic forms of stock whip.* The Raman whip was created by a South African inventor who pioneered it in Ontario in modern times.

Rape: To force sexual penetration on another person without consent. *Prisoners like to rape one another to determine social hierarchy.* Origin: Mesopotamian.

Rat Exposure: A form of **rat torture** in which a person is gutted but is then left tied up for rats to find and eat. *The problem with rat exposure is that the rats may decide to eat the ropes so the victim is freed and can escape.* Origin: ancient Roman.

Rat Chair: A chair with a cage enclosed around the person's head. The cage can be opened from the bottom, and it can also open like a normal cage from the front. Rats (or other creatures or insects) can be introduced. The rats are locked in, and they live there, eating the person's head. The person also has to live there until death. *Kaye regretted having pet rats because they ate her head and defecated and urinated on her in the rat chair instead of helping her escape.* Origin: medieval Germany.

Rat Torture: 1. To cut slits into a person's stomach and put rats inside so the person gets eaten. 2. See **cauldron**. 3. See **rat chair**. *The mad scientist's experiments involved using his pets on other people in the form of rat torture.* Origin: medieval Germany.

Red Theater: A scaffold where the guillotine is employed. *People got to watch the king of France beheaded at the red theater.* Origin: French Revolution.

Relax one in the Secular Arm: To allow local authorities to execute a heretic. *Pope Gregory IX relaxed many supposed heretics in the secular arm because there were so many of them.* Origin: Spanish Inquisition.

Religious Humiliation: To belittle or discriminate a person based off of his or her religious belief system. *The Christian Nazi force fed the Jew raw pork as a religious humiliation.* Origin: ancient Mesopotamian.

Republican Marriage: To tie naked men and naked women together and kill them both by **drowning, shooting,** or **impalement.** **Abacinating** them first was optional. *Although not attracted to each other, Marie and Antoine spent their honeymoon in the afterlife after their marriage in the river.* Origin: French Revolution.

Reverse Hanging: English for **strappado**.

Revolving Drum: A barrel covered in nails. The victim is made to lie down on it with his or her stomach, and a crank makes the drum spin. Stones are usually piled on top of the victim's back to press the person into the nails. The drum is made to spin until the victim dies of disembowelment. *The prisoner threatened to name his accusers as his coconspirators if he was interrogated by the revolving drum.* Origin: Spanish Inquisition.

Rhaphanidosis: The act of sodomizing a person with radishes for sex-related crimes, such as adultery, promiscuity, and homosexuality. Variations of Rhaphanidosis are performed with broom handles, gerbils, dildos, vibrators, butt plugs, mullet fish, eels, snakes, cords, chains, tubes, nails, ashes, Tabasco sauce, **anal pear/pear of anguish**, and anything that can fit inside the anus except for human body parts. As capital punishment, the items shoved up the anus are as rough as possible, and as many as possible are used until the person dies of internal hemorrhaging. *The adulterer was sentenced by the gay judge to death by Rhaphanidosis.* The word *Rhaphanidosis* is Greek. The idea of sodomy as a prescribed punishment originated in ancient China.

Rhinokopia: To cut off someone's nose. *Even though Justinian lost his nose to Rhinokopia, he rose to become the emperor nonetheless.* The word *Rhinokopia* is Greek; however, nose amputations originate in ancient India, and amputation of any kind came from ancient Israel.

Ride Backward up Holborn Hill: To ride in the hangman's cart to Tyburn from the Tower of London. *Robert rode backward up Holborn Hill to certain doom.* Origin: medieval England.

Riding Crop: A short **whip** that has a fiberglass shaft or cane covered in leather, fabric, or other synthetic with a thick handle at one end and a thin, flexible cord or leather strip at the other. The handle may have a leather loop that fits around the user's wrist so that he or she doesn't lose it. *The riding crop was originally designed for horses to urge them to go faster while one was riding or racing them.* Origin: medieval England.

Riding Quirt: See **quirt**.

Riding the Rail: To be tied down to a wooden beam by wrists and ankles and then to have other tortures or humiliations combined with it. As an execution, it is often accompanied by **tarring and feathering**. As corporal punishment it is combined with flogging and sexual assault. *The patient rode the rail, and the doctors tarred and feathered her.* Riding the rail is a descendant of an early version of a Roman **rack** and the **Spanish donkey** of the Inquisition. **Tarring and feathering** was invented in Colonial America.

Ritual Humiliation: To humiliate a person on a consistent basis so that he or she expects mistreatment at a certain time and the dread of it becomes a torture. *Kitty was ritually humiliated every day at midnight, and she would spend the rest of her time fruitlessly trying to escape or hide to avoid it; however, it always happened regardless.* Origin: ancient Mesopotamian.

Romal: A **Quirt** with a handle twice as long as a normal quirt. *There is no difference between a Romal and a quirt other than the longer handle. They were both used for the same purpose.* Origin: medieval England.

Rope's End: Another term for **flagellation** or **hanging**. *To be at the rope's end also meant flogging as well as hanging if the whip used was made of rope.* Origin: medieval England.

Rose Whip: A type of **stock whip** used in Canada, related to the **Raman whip**. *The rose whip is one of the more generic stock whips.* The rose whip was created in modern times by an American farmer who pioneered it in Canada.

S

Sackcloth: See **cilice**.

Sally Port: A large cage used to transport prisoners to and from prison. *The sally port is like a giant hanging cage, but it's only for temporary use by one prisoner at a time.* Origin: medieval England.

Sambok: Alternate spelling for **sjambok**.

Saw: A long, thin blade with sharp teeth used for cutting. Saws can be used to amputate body parts, to quarter or dismember, or to cut a person in half. People can be cut in half by being hung upside down with their legs spread, and the saw can cut them in half slowly from their perineum down their spines and lastly the skull. People can also be cut in half across the torso as they lie down. Alternately people can be pinned standing between two boards and cut in half from their skull down. *Isaiah was sawed in half upside down for prophesying.* Origin: ancient Hebrew.

Scaffold: The public platform where both corporal and capital punishments take place. *The scaffold was in the marketplace where people would take a break from shopping to watch people get disciplined and/or killed.* Origin: Hebrew.

Scalping: To cut off the top of a person's head. *Stupid Horse barely survived the scalping.* Origin: ancient North American.

Scalping Chair: A chair with a hole cut out for the head to rest on and another hoop just behind it. The person's hair is wrapped tightly around that hoop. The hoop is drawn back by mechanisms, pulling the hair and eventually ripping the scalp off. *The witch used the scalping chair on Rapunzel so she could not let down her hair anymore.* Origin: Spanish Inquisition.

Scaphism: See **scaphismus**.

Scaphismus: To sandwich a person between two boats, barrels, hollowed-out tree trunks, to simply put a person in a box with only his or her head sticking out and force the victim to live there, eat there, drink there, sleep there, and use the bathroom there, never allowed out. The result is that the person urinates and defecates there, and this attracts insects that eat the flesh from inside out, creating a slow disembowelment process. *Solomon died after he lived in the scaphismus for two weeks and three days.* Origin: ancient Greece.

Scavenger's Daughter: 1. A metal hoop with a large screw on top. The person kneels inside of the hoop. The screw tightens and compresses the entire body. *The scavenger's daughter compressed the man so much that he bled out of every orifice, his fingernails, and his sweat.* 2. A series of hoops connected by metal bars—one hoop around the neck, two for the wrists close to the first hoop, and two hoops for the ankles with stirrups for the soles of the feet. The person is put in an awkward sitting position, and if he or she moves, the person might break or strain whatever he or she is trying to move. *She urinated and defecated in the corner of her cell while she was confined in the scavenger's daughter.* Origin: medieval England.

Schandmantel: German for **barrel pillory**, literally translated as "coat of shame."

Schandmaske: German for shameful mask, which refers to the **mask of shame**.

Schandstenen: Dutch for **whirligig**.

Schandtome: Dutch for **barrel pillory** literally translated as "barrel of shame."

Schlimme Liesel: German for fearful Eliza, which was a nickname for the **rack**.

Scold's Bridle: Another name for **branks**.

Scottish Maiden: An ancient beheading device that looked like a painter's easel with a sharp blade attached to it. The victim's head rests where the canvas would be, and the victim would kneel between the legs behind the blade. *The Scottish Maiden was inspired by the Halifax Gibbet and was later a precursor to the guillotine.* Origin: medieval Scotland.

Scourge: An ancient **whip** with many thongs and lashes fastened to the handle. The handle and lashes were made of naval thick ropes and/or leather. *The scourge was the first whip documented in history, and its original purpose was to thresh wheat. It was the ancient Hebrews' idea to use it to whip people, and they took the scourge with them when they famously left Egypt under the leadership of Moses.* Origin is ancient Egyptian. The scourge is the first whip mentioned in documented history, and all other whips have descended from it over the centuries. The ancient Roman **cat o' nine tails** bears the closest resemblance.

Scragboy: Another word for **hangman**. The word *scrag* is old English, meaning "to throttle." *Come to Scrag'em Fair and see Scragboy scrag another miscreant with the fearsome Scrag Squeezer!* Origin: medieval England.

Scrag'em Fair: Nickname for Tyburn. *Come to Scrag'em Fair and see Scragboy scrag another miscreant with the fearsome Scrag Squeezer!* Origin: medieval England.

Scragged, Ottomised, and then Grin in a Glass Case: Old English for "hanged anatomized, or dissected and then put on display for doctors and surgeons to take note." *The miscreant was scragged, ottomised, and then grinned in a glass case after performing with Scragboy at Scrag'em Fair.* Origin: medieval England.

Scrag Squeezer: Another name for the **gallows**. *Come to Scrag'em Fair and see Scragboy scrag another miscreant with the fearsome Scrag Squeezer!* Origin: medieval England.

Scythe: A beheading or cutting implement that is a crescent-shaped blade attached to a long wooden handle. *Death is classically portrayed using a scythe to harvest mortals' souls.* Origin is ancient Mesopotamian. The scythe was originally a farming tool used to harvest wheat or other crops.

Senior Birch: See **birch**.

Sensory Deprivation: To make a person blind and/or deaf either temporary or permanent. *Sensory deprivation is more commonplace as a torture by itself in modern times than it was in medieval or ancient when this was more often combined with other punishments.* Origin: ancient Mesopotamian.

Seville Tongue Trimmer: Another term for the **tongue tearer**.

Sewn in an Animal's Carcass: The act of finding a whole animal carcass, making a vertical slit from sternum to genitalia, emptying out all organs and the skeleton, replacing those with a living human, and then stitching the slit closed so that only the person's head sticks out, leaving the victim to die inside the rotting animal. Another variant would include tying a living human to any corpse, human or animal, and leaving the person to die with the corpse rotting on top of him or her. *The Christian martyrs who were sewn into animal carcasses talked to one another as they died.* Origin: ancient Roman.

Sexual Assault: To coerce a person into performing a sex act, such as masturbating, oral sex, **naked pyramid**, or **rape**. *Prison guards sometimes sexually assault all the prisoners to remind them that the guards are on top of the social hierarchy.* Origin: ancient Mesopotamian.

Sexual Harassment: To sexually humiliate or assault a person in public, usually by teasing, groping, and love-tapping. *Eve was sexually harassed by several men and women while she was visiting India.* Origin: ancient Indian.

Sexual Humiliation: To humiliate someone sexually or with something sex-related. This can include taking naked pictures or laughing at people who are naked. This may either happen privately or publicly. *Omar was obligated to walk on an AIDS patient's blood naked as a sexual humiliation.* Origin: ancient Mesopotamian.

Shaaburg: Somali dialect for generic leather **whip**. It most commonly refers to the **Sjambok**. The Somali dialect does not appear to differentiate different types of whips.

Shackle: See **fetter**.

Shaking: To grab a person and to throttle that individual back and forth several times. This sometimes involves lifting the person up if the shaker has the strength to do that. *Getting shaken makes one dizzy.* Origin: ancient Mesopotamian.

Shaming: To make people ashamed of something they have done, usually requiring public **humiliation** or the use of a humiliation device, such as **stockades** or the like. *Shaming people is making them realize, "Look* *what you've done. You just made a laughingstock of yourself.*" Origin: ancient Mesopotamian.

Shank: A shank is a homemade knife that is actually a piece of glass, metal, or melted plastic with one end of it wrapped in cloth or tape to make a handle. This would be used to shank or **jump** someone. *Shanking is the corporal punishment form of jumping, which is intended to kill.* Origin: medieval England.

Sheriff's Picture Frame: Another name for the **gallows**. *Would you like your picture taken in Sheriff's Picture Frame? Come to Scrag'em Fair!* Origin: medieval England.

Shin Crusher: See **Iron Boot**.

Shoeing: To nail a horse's shoe into a person's foot. *The gang liked to leave their mark on people by shoeing them like horses to demean them as animals.* Origin: medieval Persia.

Show Cane: A short, stiff cane made of holly, cherry, or birch wood and may or may not be covered in leather. *The show cane was not only for show but was also a great weapon.* Origin: medieval England.

Shower Bath: A form of **Chinese water torture** in which the victim is in a seated position and has many buckets of water dumped on them continuously. *Len took the challenge to sit in the shower bath and have buckets of ice water dumped on him.* Origin: ancient China.

Shrew's Fiddle: Another word for **neck violin**.

Shunning: See **ostracizing**.

Si: Chinese for death.

Sicilian Bull: See **brazen bull**.

Sickle: Another word for **scythe**.

Signal Whip: A single-lashed three- to four-foot **whip** with no **fall**. *In a snake whip the lash attaches to the fall. In a signal whip the lash is directly attached to the body.* Origin: medieval England.

Silent Treatment: Another word for **ostracizing**.

Silla: Spanish for chair. It was quite simply an ordinary chair a person was tied down to and then beaten on the face, head, and chest by another person, most commonly with a metal pipe or similar object. *The Roman iron chair evolved into the Spanish chair of nails and has over the centuries devolved into the simple silla. Modern tortures are extremely simplistic.* Origin: modern Cuba.

Sjambok: A heavy leather whip made of hippopotamus hide, rhinoceros hide, or plastic. A strip is cut three to five feet long and is tapered so one side is thicker than the other. The thicker end becomes the handle. It is then rolled between heavy metal plates until it reaches a cylindrical form that is both flexible and durable. *Today South African police use the Sjambok for riot control and discipline, and ordinary citizens use it for cattle driving, snake killing, and self-defense.* This originates from modern South Africa. The Sjambok is a direct descendant of the Indonesian **cambuk**.

Skaple: Literally meaning "green" or "scooped out" or "hollowed out" in ancient Greek. Skaple referred to boats or tree trunks that are hollowed out. Skaple was the Greek word for **scaphismus**. *Scaphismus was called Skaple before it was brought to ancient Rome and then Persia, where the word was altered to Scaphismus.* Origin: ancient Greece.

Skeffington's Gyves: Another word for the **scavenger's daughter**.

Skinning: See **flaying**.

Skull Splitter: A metal hoop lined with spikes that encircles the person's head just above the eyes. The hoop can tighten to break into the skull and into the brain. *The skull splitter popped the top of the man's skull off, and the scientist studied his exposed brain.* This term comes from the Spanish Inquisition. The skull splitter is a descendant of the **crown of thorns**.

Slapping: To strike a person with the palm of the hand. This does not cause a lot of pain unless done repeatedly. It is mainly used to shock the victim. *Maurice liked to slap other men across the face and women across the buttocks.* Origin: ancient Mesopotamian.

Slapstick: A plank used to flog or whip people. *The popular use of the slapstick in the routines of vaudeville comedians gave rise to a genre of comedy known as slapstick comedy.* Origin: ancient Hebrew.

Slavery: Lifelong bondage or servitude to an individual or family or to whomever the slaves would be sold. Historically slaves would be used to perform menial and/or humiliating tasks daily, and most of the time they would be tortured by a variety of methods. **Flagellation** was unquestionably the most popular, but they could also be **castrated, flayed, eaten by animals, crucified, denailed,** had **teeth extracted, scalped, burned, boiled, buried alive,** locked away in a **sweatbox, ice box,** or **solitary confinement, strappado, scaphismus, bee basket, hanged, dismembered, disemboweled, stretched, compressed, force-fed, sexually** and/or **religiously humiliated, raped, sodomized, starved,** etc. They were subjected to any and all forms of physical and/or sexual torture as either punishment for small misdemeanors or simply for the sadistic pleasure of their masters. However, not all slave owners were cruel, and even if a slave was never physically or sexually assaulted, simply being a slave was psychologically humiliating. Everywhere slaves looked, they were constantly reminded of being the bottom-feeders of society and every aspect of their lives were constantly dominated by the whims of their masters or other people. Slaves can also be kept exclusively for masters to prostitute to other people, but the masters are generally the ones who get paid. *In the beginning anyone could be a slave, as it depended on one's financial or social status, whether or not one was in debt to another person, or whether or not one was kidnapped, sold into slavery by parents, or was a prisoner of war. A millennia later Victorian England made it racial and then spread it to colonial America during colonization. Nowadays in modern times children and teenagers are targeted, kidnapped, and used exclusively as sex slaves, and this is not defined by gender or race.* The etymology of the word slave derives from Slav when the Slavic people were enslaved by ancient Mongolians, but slavery itself can be traced back to ancient Mesopotamia.

Sleep Adjustment: To disrupt a person's sleep cycle by curtailing the number of hours they are allowed to sleep. *Some cults employ sleep adjustments for spiritual reasons. They could be alert for God or more appropriately, for the cult leader.* Origin: ancient Mesopotamian.

Sleep Deprivation: To make sure a person doesn't go to sleep as a punishment or interrogation technique. *If a person is deprived of sleep long enough, they will go insane and hallucinate because they have not been able to dream properly.* Origin: ancient Mesopotamian.

Sleeping with the Fishes: Modern American euphemism for **drowning** someone.

Slicing Process: Another word for **thousand cuts**.

Slippering: To beat a person by using a shoe, especially with the soles, and also to sodomize someone using the spike of a stiletto. *Mistress Bunny slippered Puppy with a slipper.* Origin: ancient Mesopotamia.

Slow Slicing: See **thousand cuts**.

Smoke Inhalation: To tie a person down in a corner so that his or her head is immobile against a wall. The torturer can then light a fire at the other end of the room. The victim is forced to breathe in the smoke and suffocate. *Smoke inhalation is a creative way to kill someone with fire without actually burning the person.* Origin: ancient China.

Snake Whip: A single-lashed four-foot-long **whip** with no handle. It is called a snake whip because it can be curled up in a circle to resemble a snake. *The cowboy's favorite kind of whip was the fast snake whip.* Origin: medieval England.

Sodomy: Sexual intercourse through the rectum as a punishment. This is a form of rape between two men or between a man and a woman. Sodomy can also take place by the dominant one using an object such as a dildo, vibrator, lubricant, and/or **rhaphanidosis**. *Although none of the prisoners or prison guards was homosexual, they were all well-acquainted with sodomy.* Origin: ancient Mesopotamian.

Solitary Confinement: To put a person in a cell, room, tower, or suite and leave the individual alone. Solitary confinement for long periods of time can lead to **starvation** and **dehydration**. *Whitney is afraid of being alone, so solitary confinement for two hours was a big punishment for her.* Origin: ancient Mesopotamian.

Sound: See **evil noise**.

Spanish Coat: See **barrel pillory**.

Spanish Boot: Another word for **iron boot**.

Spanish Chair: See **chair of nails**.

Spanish Crusher: A large metal claw that is closed by bringing together the long, heavy handles in front that draw parallel lines when closed.

The Spanish crusher pulverizes whatever is lying in the claw when it closes. Most body parts or inanimate objects can fit inside. *She destroyed a pistachio inside the Spanish crusher to demonstrate how she could use it to crush his own nuts.* Origin: Spanish Inquisition.

Spanish Donkey: A wooden wall with a sharp edge or planks. A person sits on top of this wall as though he or she is riding a donkey. Weights attached to the person's feet cause gravity to pull them down, and the person splits in two from the perineum up the body. The wall is usually accompanied by a wooden horse head and tail on the ends so the person looks like he or she is riding a donkey or horse. The Spanish donkey is also the precursor to **riding the rail**, and the plank or beam used for that is sometimes also called the Spanish donkey or wooden horse. Another version of this was a large, hollow donkey statue with a hole in the back. The person would be seated on top of it, and inside the statue was a spike that could poke out and impale the person. The spike could be made to strike out repeatedly. *The prostitute rode the Spanish donkey for three days until she was split so much her perineum dragged the ground on either side of the planks.* Origin: Spanish Inquisition.

Spanish Gaiter: See **iron boot**.

Spanish Mantle: See **barrel pillory**.

Spanish Mouth Pear: See **pear of anguish**.

Spanish Spider: Another word for **iron spider**.

Spanish Tickler: Another word for **cat's paws**.

Spear: A long staff with a piece of metal shrapnel attached to one end used to **cut** or **impale** people, usually instead of iron stakes. *Spears were originally used by Mesopotamian cavemen for the purposes of hunting animals.* Origin: ancient Mesopotamia.

Spider: 1. See **iron spider**. 2. See **wall of nails**.

Spike: A sharp metal stud or a nail. *The prankster put the spike in the teacher's chair.* Origin: ancient Mesopotamian.

Spiked Chair: See **chair of nails**.

Spiked Collar: A metal disk or collar that fits around the person's neck and is lined with spikes on the inside. Spikes may also line the outside of it to prevent the victim from taking it off. *Since medieval times, the spiked collar has devolved into a fashion statement, but without the spikes lining the inside.* Origin: Spanish Inquisition.

Spiked Punishment Collar: Same as **spiked collar**.

Spiked Torture Helmet: A helmet with a spike connected to the front and close to the wearer's mouth and a screw in the back of the head. The screw is turned, and the spike is raised up and drilled into the forehead until it cracks through the skull and into the brain, finally killing the person. *The executioner turned the screw slowly, prolonging death by the spiked torture helmet.* Origin: Spanish Inquisition.

Spiked Witch's Chair: A **chair of nails** used to interrogate men and women suspected of witchcraft. *The witch cast several spells to make herself not bleed or feel pain in the spiked witch's chair, to make it untie her, and to make it come to life and kill the persecutors.* Origin: Spanish Inquisition.

Spit: See **poker**.

Squassation: Another word for **strappado**.

Stabbing: To strike or impale someone with a **knife, spear,** or other sharp instrument. *Stabbing someone may or may not be fatal, depending on where the victim is stabbed.* Origin: ancient Mesopotamian.

Stabbed by a Bridport Dagger: To be hanged. *Doris was stabbed by a Bridport dagger in Dorset.* Origin: medieval England.

Staffman: Scottish nickname for a **hangman**. *The staffman hanged the bad man.* Origin: medieval Scotland.

Stake: A wooden pole or tree a person is tied to and then burned alive with. This is sometimes accompanied by gunpowder or a garrotte attached to it. *Joan of Arc was burned alive for clairaudience, which was considered witchcraft back then.* Origin: ancient Hebrew.

Starvation: To deny a prisoner any food so that he or she dies of hunger. *It took months for the fat lady to die of starvation.* Origin: ancient Mesopotamian.

Stick: 1. See **cudgel**. 2. See **whip**.

Stockades: A wooden board with three holes cut out from it. The person's neck fits in the center hole, and the wrists fit in the holes on either side. Stockades may be used in combination with **ankle stocks**, or other limbs may be put in the holes of the stockades, such as the head and ankles, to further increase the humiliation or provide additional discomfort. Stockades are usually paired with floggings, beatings, and sodomy or rape in private. A smaller version may be used for the male sex organs if the holes are arrayed in a closely knit triangle. A rarer version that was used in medieval England included a wooden or metal post sticking out of a wall. The person's genitals rested on the post with his or her feet off the ground and his or her hands, thumbs, or hair pinned up higher on the wall or ceiling. Another version depicted a metal disk on the ground that was large enough to keep a person kneeling in the center. The person would be tied down in a kneeling position by chains attached to the disk. The punisher would spin the disk and then flog the person as he or she spun. This version was primarily used in medieval France. *The* *felon was put in the stockades and ridiculed all day and night.* Origin: ancient Hebrew.

Stocks: Short for **stockades.**

Stock Whip: A single-lashed leather **whip** with a long lash but a short handle. *There are several different kinds of stock whips. It is one of the more varied types of whips.* The origin is Victorian Australia. It is the descendent of the British hunting whip.

Stoning: To throw or drop boulders on a person until he or she dies. Often people were incapacitated. Sometimes they were buried in the ground with only their heads visible. Sometimes those heads were covered by a sheet if the executioners didn't want to see the victims die. *The angry mob stoned the unpopular sex offender.* Origin: ancient Hebrew.

Stork: nickname for **scavenger's daughter.**

Straight Belt: A leather or wooden belt with two holes in the side that fits around a person's waist. The holes fit snuggly around the wrists. This was used to confine both prisoners and the criminally insane alike, and it was always paired with other tortures. *The madman struggled in the confines of the straight belt.* This belt comes from the Spanish Inquisition. The straight belt is also precursor to the **straitjacket.**

Straitjacket: A cloth jacket a person wears. The sleeves are often bound behind the person's back. An additional strap around the groin provides further restraint. This was used to confine both prisoners and the criminally insane alike, and it was always paired with other tortures. *The madman escaped from the straitjacket and held the nurse captive.* Origin: medieval France.

Strangulation: To crush a person's neck to silence the individual or to block the person's lungs from receiving air so that he or she dies.

One could use his or her hands or a noose, cord, necklace, belt, scarf, or similar items. **Hanging** and **garrotte** were designed to strangle a person to death. *Tyler strangled his girlfriend and killed her.* Origin: ancient Mesopotamian.

Strappado: To hang a person by the wrists. The person's wrists were tied behind his or her back so that the shoulders were dislocated. The victim may be swung, dropped, and have weights attached to their ankles for further injuries. *Strappado is still used in some parts of the world today.* Origin: Spanish Inquisition.

Strap: A leather strip used to flog or whip people. See **tawse**. *A strap is basically a whip thong used to operate by itself.* Origin: medieval Scotland.

Strapping: To flog or whip someone with a leather strap or a pair of **tawse**. *Thistle MacAllister strapped Duncan McCleaver with her tawse in self-defense.* Origin: medieval Scotland.

Streckbank: German for "stretching frame," which is their name for the **rack**.

Stress Position: To put a person in a position that is extremely uncomfortable. This includes undergoing the **scavenger's daughter, wall standing,** hanging upside down, being tied to walls or furniture, holding a big tree, standing in one place unable to move for hours or days, **curaisse, stockades, murga, body folding, taking the riding posture,** etc. *The prisoner was led to and from buildings blindfolded, bent over by the waist, and handcuffed with his hands behind his back in a stress position so he could not map out the prison in his mind.* Origin: ancient Mesopotamian.

String: Another word for **lash**.

Suffocation: To cover a person's nose and mouth so that he or she cannot breathe. **Drowning** and using smoke are popular forms, but one can also use fabric or feathers. When a person is **buried alive**, they suffocate on dirt. Suffocation using ash was common in both ancient Persia and Aztecan Mexico. *Edward and Richard's bodies showed signs that they were suffocated to death.* Origin: ancient Mesopotamian.

Suspensus per Collum: Latin for "hanged by the neck."

Swallow: To tie a person's wrists and ankles together behind the back so that his or her body is shaped like a teardrop. The person is then suspended above the ground by a crane or pulley hooked around his or her limbs. *Alena eventually died because too much blood rushed to her head because of swallow.* Origin: medieval Ukrainian.

Swallow Flying: Another name for **swallow**.

Sweatbox: A deliberately overheated room that a person is put in. The person is then left there to die of heat exhaustion. *Andy thought he was in solitary confinement, but then he realized he was in a sweatbox.* Origin: modern South America.

Sweating: Other than using a **sweatbox**, a person could be made to run around an outdoor area like the mast of a ship. This area was usually prodded with sharp instruments such as swords or bayonets. The person would run until he or she either completely collapsed from sheer exhaustion or died. Alternatively the person could be smothered by several quilts and then tied to a bed or a tree outside in the middle of a hot and sticky summer day. *Criminals were made to run laps. Sweating as a punishment was a precursor to the sweatbox.* Origin: medieval England.

Swedentrunk: Literally translated as "Swedish drink." One puts a funnel in a person's mouth and carefully pours sewer water down the victim's throat so as not to choke him or her. This is done until the person dies or becomes severely bloated, and then the person is kicked and beaten in the abdomen until death. Compare to **force-feeding**. *They lay the bondservant on the ground, stuck a wooden wedge in his mouth, and poured into his belly a bucket of foul manure water, which they called a Swedish Drink, Swedentrunk.* Origin: medieval Sweden.

Swirly: To **waterboard** a person by dunking the head in a toilet. Flushing the toilet was optional. *Roger's idea of a swirly was to almost drown someone in a plugged toilet.* Origin: modern United Kingdom.

Switch: A short stick used to whip or flog people. *Switches can be made from the branches of any tree.* Origin: ancient Celtic Britain.

Sword: A long, sharp, thin blade used for decapitation, every other form of amputation, quartering, and any other form of severe cutting and stabbing. One can also impale someone's back, stomach, or chest all the way through with a sword. *Jean-Baptiste could quickly behead a victim with one stroke of the sword.* Origin: ancient Hebrew.

T

Tablilla: To pound into a person's toes by using a hammer and chisel. *Gordon had the most difficulty walking after he was subjected to tablilla on all ten of his toes.* Origin: ancient Chinese.

Taking the Riding Posture: A **stress position** in which the victim is forced to stand as if they are riding a horse for hours. Just like with any other stress position, the victim will be beaten if he or she tries to move or cannot maintain the position the individual is expected to maintain. *It was helpful to the victim taking the riding posture to imagine riding an actual horse away from this place of misery.* Origin: ancient Mesopotamian.

Ta'liq: Chinese for "hanging from a metal bar," a form of **body suspension**.

Tarring and Feathering: To cover a person's body in hot tar or wax and then cover the victim in feathers that stick to the tar. The tar slowly burns them to death. *The pirate was tarred and feathered as he rode the rail.* Origin: colonial America.

Tattoo: To mark a person by inserting ink or other pigments under their skin to permanently mark them. In both ancient Asia and ancient Europe, criminals had their crimes tattooed on their foreheads for all to see. Slaves were also tattooed with their identification so that other people knew that they were slaves. Sometimes other phrases were used.

Fugitive, debtor, or the simple phrase "I'm a slave" were also common. The most common place for a slave tattoo was on the forehead, but hands, arms, and legs were also used. It had to be a body part that anyone looking at them would see immediately. In ancient China, one of the five punishments prescribed for slaves was **mo**, which was also called **qing** and meant "tattooed on the face or forehead with indelible ink." Tattooing was used interchangeably with **branding**, as both were used for the same purposes. Ancient Asia and Ancient Europe were the only cultures who viewed tattooing negatively. All other cultures viewed the practice positively and often with spiritual meanings. *In modern times Europe and Asia's views on tattooing have changed drastically, and both view the practice in a positive light like the rest of the world has since the dawn of humanity.* The ancient Mesopotamians were the first people to practice tattooing. The ancient Japanese were the first people to punish criminals and slaves with it, and they view the practice with prejudice.

Tawse: Leather straps used to whip people. The singular form of the word is taw, and each strap could have one or two tails at the end of the lash. *Thistle MacAllister used her tawse to defend herself against the gangsters.* Origin: medieval Scotland.

Taser: A handheld gun-shaped device that shoots out electric barbs attached to the gun by wires. The barbs give an electric shock, and pulling the trigger again will give the barbs more electricity. The barbs have to be removed from underneath the skin where they have implanted themselves, and some tasers aren't rechargeable. *Police use tasers to avoid using their gun.* Origin: modern North America.

Tean Zu: To put bamboo sticks in between and around fingers all interconnected by strings. The strings are tightened to crush the fingers between the sticks. *Tae's hand model career ended because of Tean Zu.* Origin: ancient Chinese.

Tekko: A horseshoe-shaped blade attached to a stick as a handle. The person using it punches the victim to cut the person. *Ikki was very skilled at slitting his opponent's throats with the tekko.* This originated in feudal Japan. The *tekko* was the precursor to the ancient Greek Cestus and the North American brass knuckles.

Texas Chili Bowl: The act of sodomizing a person with Tabasco sauce and a telephone cord. *The redneck served the gay kid a mean Texas chili bowl.* Origin: modern Southern United States.

Thief Catcher: See **neck grabber.**

Thong: Another word for **lash.**

Thousand Cuts: The act of randomly selecting a body part out of a thousand of possibilities and mutilating that body part and then repeating the process with different body parts until death. The body part to be mutilated, however way the executioner saw fit, was selected either by drawing from a basket pieces of paper with the names of body parts written on them or by drawing from a basket knives or other implements with the names of body parts written on the blade. *Executioner Ping boasted that he could make the process of a thousand cuts last a hundred days if he wanted.* Origin: ancient Mongolia.

Threat: To tell other people that they will suffer either or both physical or psychological harm for something they did or didn't do. *The blackmailer threatened to expose them if they called the police.* Origin: Mesopotamian.

Throat Slitting: To sever the carotid arteries in the neck with one quick stroke of a knife or other cutting implement. *The killer preferred to dispatch his victims with throat slitting because they died quickly.* Origin: medieval England.

Thrown from a Cliff: To throw someone off a cliff or a great height. The death may either be quick and painless or very painful, lasting for days depending on how the victim lands or is rolled down. *Aesop was thrown off a cliff for stealing treasure from Apollo's temple.* Origin: ancient Greece.

Thumbikins: Scottish nickname for **thumbscrews**.

Thumbscrew: 1. A small metal press that a person's hand or fingers fit through. The press tightens, crushing those body parts. 2. Two rows of bars interconnected. Fingers fit through these bars, and the device can be tightened. 3. Metal rings on the arm of a chair that the hand fits through and the torturer can squeeze. *The violinist couldn't play anymore because of the thumbscrews.* Origin: Spanish Inquisition.

Tickle Torture: To tickle the soles of the feet or other sensitive places, doing so continuously for hours at a time. *Penelope pissed her pants several times while she submitted to Mistress T's tickle tortures.* Origin: ancient Chinese.

Tied in a Sack with Animals: To be put in a large sack with dangerous animals, the most common being dogs, roosters, poisonous snakes, and gorillas. The is bag tied, and then it is thrown into a river where either the person was mauled or eaten to death or drowned. The animals would all drown. *Magrus was tied in a sack with animals and thrown in a river immediately after confessing to matricide.* Origin: ancient Roman.

Tiger Cage: cramped, cagelike prison cell that can house four people at a time. It is called a tiger cage because it is big enough to fit a tiger inside, but it is only for people. *The four best friends tried to escape from the tiger cage before noon.* Origin: modern Vietnamese.

Toe Breaker: A type of **foot press** with a drill. It drills holes into the foot, normally into the toes. *Toby's toes broke in the toe breaker.* Origin: Spanish Inquisition.

Tongue Shredder: See **tongue tearer.**

Tongue Stretcher: A chair with a **mouth opener** attached to it and another iron hoop or press that clamps down on the person's tongue. The mechanism moves away and stretches out the tongue until it swells so much that the person chokes to death. It can also be combined with the **tongue tearer.** *The politician who often lied to people was put in the tongue stretcher and was executed by choking on his own tongue.* Origin: Spanish Inquisition.

Tongue Tearer: A device resembling a small pair of scissors combined with a pair of pliers. The tongue tearer was used to reach inside a person's mouth and rip out the tongue. Alternately the tongue tearer was also used to split the tongue into two or several ribbons. *The tongue tearer split the punk woman's tongue so it was forked like a snake's.* Origin: Spanish Inquisition.

Toothbrush: The everyday household item that most people use to clean their teeth can also be used as sticks put between fingers to break them as in **tean zu.** Alternatively one can use the bristles to scrub away skin in sensitive areas, such as the soles of the feet and the genitals of either a man or a woman. *Using a toothbrush to scrub away skin requires the same motion one uses for brushing teeth, only much, much harder.* Using a toothbrush as a torture device has only been documented in modern China.

Tooth Extraction: To use a pair of pliers to pull teeth out. *The Nazi dentist extracted the Jews' teeth for their gold.* Origin: medieval Germany.

Tophet: A place where people, infants, and children were burned to death as a form of execution, human sacrifice, or both. The place would have a large bronze statue of a humanoid creature with arms extended outward in supplication. The person would lie on the arms while a fire, which raged below the victim, would burn him or her to death—that is, unless the person fell into the fire or fell on the ground.

The victim would die of exposure since no one was allowed to help the person. *The parents watched their chosen children burn in the Tophet.* Origin: ancient Canaan.

Torch: A cudgel or stick lit on fire can be used for burning a person either by directly applying it to the victim or to something like a **stake, brazier, brazen bull,** etc. *Every member of the angry mob carried a torch and a pitchfork.* Origin: ancient Mesopotamian.

Town Square: The center of a city or village that is commonly used as a **scaffold** because it is the most public place to punish or execute criminals. *People driving in the town square would glimpse another criminal being punished or killed on their way to wherever they were going.* Origin: ancient Mesopotamian.

Tramp Chair: A one-man prison cell consisting of a chair surrounded by a closed cage, used mainly on vagabonds, drunks, prostitutes, and anyone else associated with the word tramp. *The tramp chair is a cross between a ducking stool and a hanging cage.* Origin: colonial America.

Tree Tearer: To bend two adjacent trees down and tie a victim's ankles to each of these. Then one lets the trees spring back in their natural positions, hopefully ripping the victim in half. *Sinnis's favorite execution method was the tree tearer because blood would always rain on him and anyone else standing nearby.* Origin: ancient Greece.

Trident: A three-pronged impaling implement similar to a **pitchfork.** *Neptune and Poseidon are often depicted as using tridents.* This instrument originated in ancient Mesopotamian. Other than pitching hay on a farm, tridents were also used to spear fish, which was why mythical figures associated with water are usually portrayed with tridents.

Tsirushi: Japanese for "hanging upside down." The victim's ankle would be tied in a noose and hanged. The top half of the victim's body would be buried. An arm was left unharmed, however, so he or she could signal confession or flip the interrogators off. Victims most often suffocated to death on the dirt or ran out of oxygen underground. *Western interpretations of Tsirushi call for the victim to be hung upside down by both ankles from the ceiling of a torture chamber. Other tortures can be used in combination with it.* Origin: feudal Japan.

Thong: Another word for **lash**.

Three-legged Mare: See **triple tree**.

To Look Over the Wood at St. James': To stand in a pillory. *Stan looked over the wood at St. James' and saw his parents standing there, shaking their heads in shame.* Origin: medieval England.

Topping Cove: Medieval slang for an executioner. *Topping* meant *beheading*, as in "cutting off the top part of a person's body," which would signal the head. *The jolly old topping cove topped some people today.* Origin: medieval England.

Torture: To put a person in a vulnerable or helpless position and to hurt the person in some way. Generally victims of torture are not able to defend themselves. Torture may be either physical, psychological, or both. *There are thousands of methods for torture.* Origin: ancient Mesopotamian.

Torturer: A person who tortures other people as either punishment, interrogation, or some pleasure. *The torturer was well-versed in many different torture methods.* Origin: ancient Mesopotamian.

Treadmill: A conveyor belt a person is expected to walk or run on. The person would be goaded with whips. The first treadmill had spikes randomly set on the moving parts to injure the soles of the person's feet as he or she walked or ran. The person would be made to run or walk miles as though they were a hamster in a wheel. *Nowadays treadmills are used as exercise equipment people trepidate themselves to, but without the spikes.* Origin: medieval England.

Triple Tree: A gallows with three arms to hang multiple victims. *Twelve people could swing from the triple tree at a time.* Origin: medieval England.

Tu: Chinese for "penal servitude" as in **community service**. There were five degrees of severity in ancient China—one year plus fifty lashes from a big stick, one and a half years plus seventy lashes, two years plus eighty lashes, two and a half years plus ninety lashes, and three years plus one hundred lashes. *Pong-ho the serf suffered the maximum humiliations prescribed in Tu.* Origin: ancient Chinese.

Tub: See **scaphismus**.

Tucker Telephone: To wrap a telephone cord around a man's genitals or a woman's breasts and then to string the same cord around a big toe and electrocute the person. *Tucker telephone could also be used on a woman's genitals with the use of a genital clamp specially designed for the clitoris and labia.* Origin: modern Vietnam.

Tumbril: Another word for the executioner's cart. *Tucker rode the tumbril to the triple tree.* Origin: medieval England.

Tunica Molesta: Latin for "annoying shirt." *Tunica molesta* is a large tunic made of flammable cloth. The cloth is lit on fire, and the person wearing it burns to death quickly. *The fashionista loved the beautiful fire print on the tunica molesta until she realized it was actually on fire.* Origin: ancient Roman.

Turned Off: To remove the ladder or stool where a hanging victim stands so that he or she can be hanged. *Clive was turned off simply because* *the scenario of being executed by hanging became too much for him.* Origin: medieval England.

Twenty-Four Cuts: A condensed version of the **thousand cuts.** The victim was cut twenty-four times by a knife in this order: one for each eyebrow, one for the fleshy part on the top of each shoulder, one for each breast or pectoral muscle, one for the flesh of each forearm, one for the flesh of each bicep, one for cutting off each thigh, one for each calf muscle, one for the heart, one for the head, one for each hand, one for each arm, one for each foot, and one for each leg cut off from the hips. The victim would never be forced to eat the severed body parts. *Even though the executioner was asked to deliver the twenty-four cuts like a butcher, he still did it very slowly over a period of days like the skilled artist he was.* Origin: ancient Mongolia.

Tyburn Blossom: Hanging victim. *Thumper the thief ripened into the Tyburn blossom fruit of the deadly nevergreen tree.* Origin: medieval England.

Tyburn Tippet: A noose. The term comes from the fact that a tippet is an old-fashioned collar women wore. *Lady Anne wore the fashionable Tyburn tippet to the festival at Scrag'em Fair.* Origin: medieval England.

Tyburn Tree: Gallows. *Little Billy climbed the Tyburn tree while the Tyburn blossom grew.* Origin: medieval England.

U

Urophagia: The act of forcing or coercing someone to drink urine. Compare to **coprophagia** and **menstrualphagia**. *Seeking an alternative to urophagia, the prisoner asked, "What am I going to drink? You can't let me die of thirst!" They replied, "You got piss, don't you?"* Origin: ancient Mesopotamia.

V

Vanus: To slit a woman's perineum so her vagina opening and anus become one large hole. *Vanuses can occur naturally during childbirth, but it was a punishment prescribed for abortion.* Origin: ancient Persia.

Veglia: 1. Literally means *awakener* in Italian. It is their word for the **Judas cradle**. It was called this because the victim couldn't sleep because the person was held in an upright position and had to contract certain muscles to avoid injury. If these people relaxed, they were impaled. 2. A device very similar to the previous version of Judas cradle except it involves a series of spikes instead of a pyramid. *Tommaso endured the Veglia so he would be declared insane and not be burned at the stake.* Origin: medieval Italy.

Veil: See **hooding**.

Veille: French for "night watch," which is their name for the **Judas cradle**. It was called this because the victim couldn't sleep because the person was held in an upright position and couldn't relax with certain muscles contracted because of the impalement.

Venetian Foot Screw: A **foot press** that has spikes lined in the upper bar and possibly in the lower bar as well. *Valentine vomited from having his foot squeezed in the Venetian Foot Screw.* Origin: medieval Italian.

Vice: See **vise**.

Vise: This work tool used to hold objects in place while work was done. It can also be used to **crush** body parts, such as hands, fingers, feet, ankles, and heads. *Some devices used for the purpose of crushing body parts tend to look like vises.* Origin: ancient Mesopotamia.

Violation: To disregard a person's human rights and/or privacy. *The most extreme form of violation is rape.* Origin: ancient Mesopotamia.

Violence: The use of physical force of any kind to punish someone either corporally or capitally, depending on the strength of force. *They say that violence doesn't solve anything, but it solves crime and makes criminals do time.* Origin: ancient Mesopotamia.

Violet Ray: A type of **taser** that uses thirty-five to sixty-five volts. A plastic wand encases the transformer, and it can be used directly or indirectly. It can also be used to brand victims as well as electrocute them. It does not produce a large amount of ultraviolet light, which is contrary to popular belief. *The violet ray was originally used medically in electrotherapy.* Origin: modern United States.

Violet Wand: A more modern version of the **Violet Ray**. See also **taser** or **picana**.

Virgin of Nuremburg: Another nickname for the **iron maiden**. Nuremburg is a city in Germany. The iron maiden was modeled after the Virgin Mary from the Bible and what medieval artists speculated she looked like.

W

Walking Stocks: 1. A board with a chain and with three holes in it, one for the head and the other two for the wrists. The person wears the board, and the chain is use to lead him or her to places like a dungeon or place of execution. 2. See **neck violin**. *People laughed and threw things at him as he was paraded in the walking stocks.* Origin: medieval Germany.

Walking the Green Mile: To walk from one's cell on **death row** to the **electric chair**. It was called this because the floor in the room of the electric chair used to be painted green. *The distance covered may or may not have been a mile long, just like the thousand cuts may or may not have been exactly a thousand. Usually it's a lot less, but it's enough to strike fear into the heart of the felon.* Origin: modern United States.

Wall Standing: To make people press the front halves of their bodies against a wall with their hands high above their heads and their feet perched up on their toes as high as possible. Alternatively a person could be obliged to stand in one place without moving for hours. This is a **stress position**. *Curtis was forced into a wall-standing position for twenty-four hours.* Origin: modern United Kingdom.

Wand: Another word for **whip**.

Wartenberg Wheel: A band used to bind the two big toes together. This is similar to Chinese finger cuffs, except a Wartenberg wheel is usually controlled by a lock and key. *Thinking that the Wartenberg wheel was the same as a Chinese finger cuff, Rhiannon struggled to escape it by pressing her two big toes together.* Origin: medieval Germany.

Water: A chemical compound consisting of hydrogen and oxygen that is a generally transparent, odorless, and tasteless liquid. Other than **waterboarding, Chinese water torture,** and the **ducking stool,** the best way to torture someone with this universal tool is to have a person or group of people locked in a room or tower that slowly fills up with water. Since they cannot escape, they know their imminent death by drowning is coming. *Hector climbed the ladder to the very top of the tall room in hopes of avoiding the water; however, there was no escape, and he drowned up there.* Origin: ancient Mesopotamia.

Waterboarding: To submerge a person's face into water, to pour water on top of the person, or to pour small streams or droplets on a person's forehead and allow him or her to get progressively heavier. Waterboarding may be a form of either corporal or capital punishment and is usually accompanied by **hooding.** Another form of water torture very similar to **Swedentrunk** was to shove a cloth tube as deeply and roughly down the victim's throat, careful not to choke the person immediately. Then the tube was filled slowly with water. It expanded to choke the victim the way the executioner intended it. *The cult leader had his newest member waterboarded as a part of his brainwashing techniques.* Origin is ancient Chinese. Waterboarding is sometimes called Chinese water torture for that reason.

Water Cure: See **waterboarding.**

Water Torture: See **waterboarding.**

Wax: The sticky yellow substance made by bees. When heated, it can be very painful to touch. A person's body can be covered in hot wax, and it can be used in place of tar or pitch in **tarring and feathering** or

cropping. Pouring hot wax down someone's throat or up the rectum or vagina will burn the person internally and will most likely kill him or her. Hot wax in the eyes will abacinate a person. Hot wax down the ears will cause a person to become permanently deaf. Wax that wasn't heated was used to cover a person's body to attract insects in the hopes he or she would be bitten and stung. This was used either by itself as **exposure** in the hot sun or used in similar ways (**hanging cage/gibbet, cyphon,** and **scaphismus**). *The use of hot wax in ancient tortures and executions has since devolved into a cosmetic hair removal treatment many women and some men use on hairy body parts today.* Origin: ancient Egyptian.

Weapon: Things used for violence, such as knives, swords, axes, whips, flails, morning stars, cat's paws, etc. Others are used in combat and are designed to cause bodily harm. Anything that can be used as a weapon can also be used as a torture device. *People say that anything can be a weapon. By that same logic anything can be used as a torture device if the person cannot defend him or herself.* Origin: ancient Mesopotamian.

Wheel: 1. A large wheel over which a person is tied. Then the person is brutally beaten to death. *The martyr was tied to the wheel, and after he was thoroughly broken, he had his body intertwined inside the spokes. Then he was left outside to die of exposure.* 2. A large wheel a person is tied to. Then the person is dismembered by being stretched around the circumference, burnt, or run over on top of spikes or on the road around the city, village, or arena. *The wheel rode on the victim all through town and off the cliff.* Origin: ancient Roman.

Whip: A strip of leather, cord, or cable attached to a handle and used to beat people as either corporal or capital punishment depending on the type of whip or type of beating. There are many different types of whips. *Without his whip, the overseer was quickly overrun by his slaves.* Origin: ancient Egyptian.

Wicker Man: A large humanoid-shaped **gibbet** or **hanging cage** that is designed to house approximately twenty to fifty people inside. It is completely made out of wood, and it is set on fire, burning the people inside. *If people are inside the wicker man's head, they will most likely suffocate on the smoke before they either get burned or the structure collapses.* Origin: ancient Celtic Britain.

Widow: Nickname for **guillotine** because it created widows out of many wives. *As the blade fell down, the widow claimed the life of yet another married man.* Origin: French Revolution.

Witch Catcher: A spear with a hook sticking out near the head. The hook would pin a person's arm behind the back, and the spear point would poke the person in the spine so that one could lead him or her forward or to the side. The hook was pulled sharply behind the person if he or she were made to walk backward. *The witch catcher was invented to use against supposed witches because it was believed that if a witch touched another person, the witch would then have power over that person.* Origin: Spanish Inquisition.

Wolf Collar: Another term for a **spiked collar**.

Wooden Collar: A large wooden collar that is secured around a person's neck and weighted. It was used as a humiliation device. *The wooden collar eventually became a metal one and then a spiked punishment collar.* Origin: medieval Germany.

Wooden Horse: A beam a person lies on after straddling it. The person is tied to ropes that pull from below and stretches the person. Alternatively the person may be situated below the rail on the ground, and the ropes could lift the person upward. The person is then stretched as he or she reaches closer to the beam. This is an early version of the **rack**, and a reinterpretation of the first position the person is in, straddling the rail, gave birth to the **Spanish donkey** and

riding the rail, which is also called the wooden horse. *Two people cannot be stretched by the wooden horse simultaneously from both on top and below.* Origin: ancient Roman.

Wooden House: A small wooden house with no windows and only one door. The person or people are put inside, and then the house is set on fire so the person(s) either burn to death or suffocate on the smoke. *People who had the bubonic plague in Europe were rounded up and put in wooden houses to be burned in hopes of stopping the disease.* Origin: medieval France.

Wooden Rosary: A rosary made of wood that a secular person was supposed to wear so other people would know the person had not been attending church, had fallen asleep during service, had disrupted service, or had left service. It was a humiliation device. *Clergymen wear rosaries with plastic beads and metal crosses; however, people can tell a person is not a clergyman if he is wearing a wooden rosary.* Origin: medieval Germany.

Wooden Ruff: See **stockades**.

Wryneck Day: Literally means "hanging day." Wryneck comes from the words *awry* and *neck*. Awry means "to one side." so the whole expression means "neck hanging to one side." *Wryneck day was usually Friday, and it was also called Hangman's Day.* Origin: medieval England.

X

Xiaoshou: Chinese for **beheading**.

Xing Chong: Chinese for "offender forced to grind grain." *Xing Chong is really a specific form of community service. The rest of the village benefits from the grain, and a bad person gets punished without payment at the same time.* Origin: ancient China.

Y

Yi: Chinese for nose amputation. See **rhinokopia**.

Yinxing: Chinese for castration. This was applied to both men and women.

Yue: Chinese for "removal of one or both feet and/or kneecaps."

Z

Zanxing: See **tean zu**.

Zanzhi: Another word for **tean zu**.

Zhang: Chinese for "beatings with a large stick." There were five degrees of this torture—sixty strokes, seventy strokes, eighty strokes, ninety strokes, and a hundred strokes. *Zing wasn't sure what degree of Zhang he wanted to administer.* Origin: ancient Chinese.

Zhangxing: Chinese for "beatings with wooden staves."

ABOUT THE AUTHOR

Nigette M. Spikes is a researcher and torture historian who has spent years compiling historical facts to create *Dictionary of Torture*. Nigette is currently working on her next project, *Encyclopedia of Torture*. She lives with her three dogs, Cody, Sara, and Sam, in Bemidji, Minnesota.